STAYCATION IN MINNESOTA: UP NORTH

What Is a Staycation?

A blend of the words "stay" and "vacation," a staycation is a day trip or mini-vacation near home. And whether you prefer your getaway to be more laid back or a tad more adventurous, there's no better place to take a staycation than Minnesota. With this book, you'll find loads of tips and suggestions for memorable trips close to home.

STAYCATION IN MINNESOTA

Up North

Patricia A. Overson

Enjoy!

Patricia A. Overson

NORTH STAR PRESS OF ST. CLOUD, INC.
St. Cloud, Minnesota

Disclaimer: While the author has made every effort to provide accurate information at the time of publication, neither the publisher nor the author assumes any responsibility for errors or for changes that occur after publication. Also, these staycations are suggestions, not necessarily recommendations.

Book cover design by Jon Flor at Dave's Great Ad Shop
Bloomington, Minnesota
www.davesgreatadshop.com

ISBN-13: 978-0-87839-416-6

First Edition: May 2011

Printed in the United States of America

Published by
North Star Press of St. Cloud, Inc.
P.O. Box 451
St. Cloud, Minnesota 56302

www.northstarpress.com

INTRODUCTION

Enjoy relaxing in scenic Northern Minnesota, where prairie meets North Woods and there is something for everyone.

They don't call Minnesota the "Land of 10,000 Lakes" for nothing. Northern Minnesota is home to some of the state's largest and most legendary lakes, including this nation's largest body of fresh water—Lake Superior! It is also home to the Boundary Waters Canoe Area Wilderness, over one million acres of pristine lakes and woods.

Among the forests and lakes, there are many outdoor activities for vacationers of all ages to enjoy in all four seasons:

- Camping at modern or rustic campsites
- Biking and hiking on miles and miles of trails
- Golfing beautiful courses
- Skiing, snowshoeing, and snowmobiling
- Visiting state parks and forests
- Thrilling to entertaining theme parks

There's also plenty for those who like their fun indoors:

- Eclectic gift shopping
- Casinos
- Museums and historic sites
- Relaxing places to stay from rustic cabins to luxury resorts
- Scrumptious restaurants
- Factory tours
- Brewery and winery visits

You can wander off the beaten path and discover:

- Scenic byways
- Roadside landmarks and oddities
- Excursions by boat or rail

In addition, you'll find a variety of lodging options:

- Bed and breakfast inns
- Hotels and motels
- Resorts
- Spiritual and educational retreats

Whether you prefer a getaway that's a little more laid back or something a tad more adventurous, there's no better place to take a fabulous staycation than Northern Minnesota.

In *Staycation in Minnesota: Up North*, you'll find loads of tips and suggestions for memorable day trips and short trips close to home.

CONTENTS

THINGS TO DO

THINGS TO SEE

WHERE TO EAT AND DRINK

WHERE TO STAY

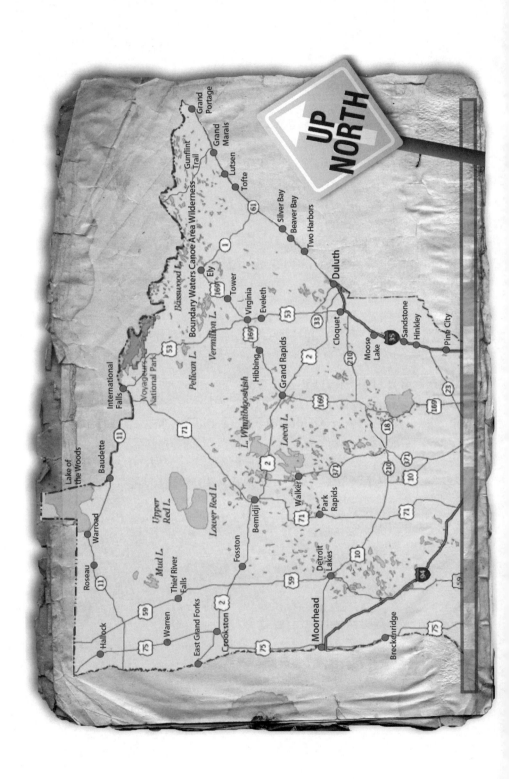

Amusement Parks, Water Parks, Theme Parks, and Zoos

The American Bear Association's
Vince Shute Wildlife Sanctuary
12541 Nett Lake Road, Orr, MN 55771
218-757-0172 • www.americanbear.org

Amenities: An expanded, raised observation deck lets visitors observe and photograph black bears in the wild. About eighty bears visit each season. The sanctuary has 360 acres of habitats, including forest, swamp, marsh, stream, and meadow, with other wildlife such as deer, bald eagles, beavers, bobcats, owls, and songbirds.

Features you'll appreciate: Shuttle from parking lot to the viewing platform, naturalist talks, and gift shop. Photography workshops offered.

Directions: About thirty minutes from Orr. From US Highway 53 about one mile south of Orr, go west at the Dam restaurant 13.3 miles on County Road 23 (Nett Lake Road). Pass County Road 514 and continue for 0.1 miles until you see the Vince Shute Wildlife Sanctuary sign on your right. Turn on the gravel road just beyond the sign and follow it for about one mile to the parking lot.

Seven Clans Casino & Water Park, Thief River Falls
20595 Center Street E., Thief River Falls, MN 56701
800-881-0712 • www.sevenclanscasino.com/page/rtf_amenities

Amenities: Four large water slides, three starter slides, wading pool, shooting geysers, water spray guns, and giant water-dumping bucket.

Features you'll appreciate: Arcade, snack shop, and gift shop.

Directions: About ten miles southeast of Thief River Falls off US Highway 59 on County Road 3 E. (Center Street E.)

North American Bear Center
1926 US Highway 169, Ely, MN 55731
218-365-7879 or 877-365-7879•www.bear.org

Amenities: Indoor and outdoor viewing of live black bears in natural habitat with a pond and waterfalls. The two-acre enclosure is home to three resident bears. More than fifty video exhibits of wild Minnesota bears, a wide variety of daily programs, and a hands-on children's area.
Features you'll appreciate: The center is air conditioned and handicapped accessible, and it has a large parking lot with plenty of room for RVs and buses.
Directions: One mile west of Ely along US Highway 169.

International Wolf Center
1396 US Highway 169, Ely, MN 55731
218-365-4695 or 800-359-9653•www.wolf.org

Amenities: Interpretive center with 1.25-acre enclosure so visitors can observe resident wolves. Interactive 6,000-square-foot "Wolves and Humans" exhibit and "Little Wolf" children's exhibit. Many naturalist and education programs, including learning vacations, wolf seminars, and adventurous field trips.
Features you'll appreciate: The center's mission is to "advance the survival of wolf populations by teaching about wolves, their relationship to wild lands, and the human role in their future."
Directions: A quarter-mile northeast of Ely on US Highway 169.

Putt-n-Go Amusement Park
1915 Highway Avenue NW, Bemidji, MN 56601
218-751-7333•www.puttngo.com

Amenities: Water slide, batting cages, go-karts, bumper boats, and miniature golf.

Features you'll appreciate: Billed as the largest water slide in Northern Minnesota: smooth-riding fiberglass flume; heated water pool; curves, drops, and tunnel; patented safe curves splashdown entry system. Showers and changing rooms.

Directions: Just off US Highway 71 N., turn right at Anne Street NW and take the first right onto Hannah Avenue NW, then take the first right onto Highway Avenue NW.

Paul Bunyan's Animal Land
3857 Animal Land Drive SE, Bemidji, MN 56601
218-759-1533•www.paulbunyansanimalland.com

Amenities: Bills itself as Minnesota's largest wildlife park and petting zoo. One hundred animals represent every continent and include lions, tigers, bears, camels, lemurs, kangaroos, monkeys, cougars, deer, llamas, reptiles, exotic birds, and bugs.

Features you'll appreciate: Indoor learning center, gift shop, picnic areas, playground, RV parking, wheelchair and stroller accessible, birthday parties, group rates, and traveling educational programs.

Directions: On US Highway 2 between Bemidji and Cass Lake.

Iron Range Off-Highway Vehicle Recreation Area
7196 Pettit Road, Gilbert, MN 55741
218-748-2207 • www.dnr.state.mn.us/ohv/trail_detail.html?id=13

Amenities: Former mining site features thirty-six miles of off-highway vehicle trails on 1,200 acres that contain iron ore pits, ore stockpiles, and tailings basins. Recreational trails, challenge areas, training, and special events.

Features you'll appreciate: Vehicles must display an off-highway vehicle registration (good for three years). Gas, restrooms, food, hotels, and campgrounds nearby.

Directions: East of Gilbert on Minnesota Highway 135; entrance is on Enterprise Trail.

Hibbing Raceway
1799 23rd Street, Hibbing, MN 55746
218-929-1150 or 218-262-2324 • http://hibbingraceway.com

Amenities: Clay track stock car racing mid-May to Labor Day; grandstand seating for 3,500; accessible to disabled.

Features you'll appreciate: Free parking. Admission free for children under twelve.

Directions: East of US Highway 169 on 23rd Street at the former St. Louis County Fairgrounds.

Character Challenge Course Company
13218 County Road 40, Park Rapids, MN 56470
218-760-8442 • www.characterchallengecourse.com

Amenities: High and low ropes challenge courses opened in 2010, featuring obstacles up to thirty-five feet in the air, giant swing, and zip line. Facilitated team-building and leadership activities for groups, families, and individuals.

Features you'll appreciate: The course is adjacent to picturesque Eagle Beach Resort.
Directions: Seven miles north of Park Rapids on US Highway 71 and one mile east on County Road 40.

Edgewater Resort & Waterpark
2400 London Road, Duluth, MN 55812
218-728-3601 or 800-777-7925 • www.duluthwaterpark.com

Amenities: Tiki Thriller: four-and-a-half story body slide. Tiki Tumbler: four-and-a-half story tube slide. Splash in Paradise Playground: Six-inch-deep slides, crazy climbing, and a 300-gallon splashdown every few minutes. Vortex: Minnesota's first vortex pool. River's Edge: 400 feet of lazy floating. Paradise Cove: 2,000-square-foot arcade with more than forty games.
Features you'll appreciate: Outdoor play area, party packages, and resort lodging, dining, and gift shop on site.
Directions: On Minnesota Highway 61 N. (London Road) twenty-four blocks north of downtown Duluth, or just off Interstate 35 at Exit 258.

Great Lakes Aquarium
353 Harbor Drive, Duluth, MN 55802
218-740-3474 • www.glaquarium.org

Amenities: This freshwater aquarium features animals and habitats from the Great Lakes Basin. Includes such exhibits as "Amazing Amazon," "Masters of Disguise," "Otter Cove," and "Freshwater Forest." Daily interpretive programs allow visitors to watch resident animals eat, play, or interact with staff.
Features you'll appreciate: The mission of the nonprofit aquarium, which opened in 2000, is to "inspire stewardship, understanding, and

exploration of the Great Lakes and their interconnection with global ecosystems."

Directions: In downtown Duluth off Interstate 35 at Exit 256B (Fifth Avenue W./Lake Avenue); west on N. Lake Avenue, right on E. Second Street and right on N. Second Avenue E.

Vertical Endeavors Indoor Rock Climbing Facility
329 Lake Avenue S., Duluth, MN 55802
218-279-9980•www.verticalendeavors.com/duluth

Amenities: Billed as the North Shore's largest climbing facility with 14,000 square feet of climbing surface and three different types of Nicros climbing walls with walls up to forty-two feet high. It has thirty top ropes, lead climbing, twelve auto belays, and a large bouldering cave.

Features you'll appreciate: Indoor and outdoor classes, pro shop, party packages, team-building programs, and homeschool days.

Directions: In the Canal Park area on the Duluth waterfront, just off Interstate 35 near Exit 256B (Fifth Avenue W./Lake Avenue).

The Encounter
201 E. First Street, Duluth, MN 55802
218-722-9820•www.encounteryfc.com

Amenities: Indoor skateboard park and youth center; music in the Red Room (local artists) and the Main Stage (nationally touring Christian artists); open gym with basketball, volleyball, and billiards; skateboard and music lessons.

Features you'll appreciate: Two coffee bars; skate and bike church; facilities available for receptions, conferences, and large events.

Directions: In downtown Duluth off Interstate 35 at Exit 256B (Fifth Avenue W./Lake Avenue); west on N. Lake Avenue, right on E. Second Street and right on N. Second Avenue E.

Lake Superior Zoo & Zoological Society
7210 Fremont Street, Duluth, MN 55807
218-730-4900 or 218-730-4500•www.lszoo.org

Amenities: Hundreds of native animals and exotic species in 16.5-acre zoo on a hillside in Fairmont Park, including African lions, Siberian tigers, polar bear, snow leopards, and Alaskan grizzly bear. Has Australian Connection (kangaroos and kookaburras), seal training shows, animal feedings, barnyard animals, primates, and nocturnal creatures. Many camps, classes, and special events.

Features you'll appreciate: Zoo train, Tiger's Paw Gift Shop, and Safari Café. Open year round except for Thanksgiving Day, Christmas Day, and New Year's Day.

Directions: From Interstate 35 northbound, take Exit 251A (Cody Street); right on N. 63rd Avenue W. to Grand Avenue; right at S. 72nd Avenue W.

Biking and Hiking Trails

Lake Bronson State Park
3793 230th Street (County Road 28), Lake Bronson, MN 56734
218-754-2200•www.dnr.state.mn.us/state_parks/lake_bronson/trails.html

Amenities: Fourteen miles of easy hiking trail along prairie and aspen parklands. Two miles of paved bike trail and five miles of mountain bike trail.
Features you'll appreciate: Two miles of handicapped accessible trail and one-half mile of self-guided interpretive trail.
Directions: Two miles east of the town of Lake Bronson with park access on County Highway 28.

Hayes Lake State Park
48990 County Road 4, Roseau, MN 56751
218-425-7504•www.dnr.state.mn.us/state_parks/hayes_lake/trails.html

Amenities: Thirteen miles of hiking along a wooded trail and five miles of mountain biking starting at Hayes Dam.
Features you'll appreciate: Two self-guided trails totaling two-and-a-half miles. Pine Ridge Interpretive trail goes from the campground to the main picnic area and the History Trail starts at Hayes Dam.
Directions: Fifteen miles south of Roseau on Minnesota Highway 89, then nine miles east on County Road 4.

Franz Jevne State Park
10218 E. Minnesota Highway 11, Birchdale, MN 56629
218-783-6252•www.dnr.state.mn.us/state_parks/franz_jevne/index.html

Amenities: Two-and-a-half miles of hiking trails.
Features you'll appreciate: Franz Jevne State Park now has an official hiking club trail along the river.
Directions: East of Birchdale on Minnesota Highway 11.

Rainy Lake Bike Trail

c/o 301 Second Avenue, International Falls, MN 56649
800-325-5766 or 218-283-9400 • www.rainylake.org

Amenities: Twelve miles of bike trail from International Falls to Rainy Lake.

Features you'll appreciate: Trail can be used for bicyclists, walkers, and inline skaters.

Directions: Trailhead one-fourth mile east of Convention and Visitors Bureau office, 301 Second Avenue, in downtown International Falls.

Arrowhead State Trail

650 US Highway 169, Tower, MN 55790
651-296-6157 or 218-753-2580, ext. 250
www.dnr.state.mn.us/state_trails/arrowhead/index.html

Amenities: 135-mile trail, with sixty-nine miles suitable for horseback riding, mountain biking, and hiking in the summer. The northern part of the trail is relatively flat between International Falls and the Ash River but the southern part has rolling hills with numerous lakes and streams, and some areas of exposed rock and enormous boulders.

Features you'll appreciate: The Arrowhead State Trail intersects with the Taconite State Trail just west of Lake Vermilion.

Directions: The trail stretches from ten miles west of Tower at the intersection of the Taconite Trail to Ericsburg, ten miles south of International Falls. Communities include Tower, Cook, Orr, and International Falls.

Taconite State Trail
Grand Rapids to Ely
www.dnr.state.mn.us/state_trails/taconite/index.html

Amenities: 165 miles of natural surface trail. The first six miles from Grand Rapids are paved for biking and inline skating. The rest of the trail is used primarily for snowmobiling in the winter, with some portions suitable for hiking, mountain biking, and horseback riding in summer.
Features you'll appreciate: Eight trail waysides and picnic areas. The trail links three state parks: Bear Head Lake, Soudan Underground Mine, and McCarthy Beach, and intersects with the Arrowhead State Trail just west of Lake Vermilion.
Directions: The trail begins on the northeast side of Grand Rapids and passes through the communities of Side Lake, Tower, and Ely.

Bear Head Lake State Park
9301 Bear Head State Park Road, Ely, MN 55731
218-365-7229
www.dnr.state.mn.us/state_parks/bear_head_lake/trails.html

Amenities: Seventeen miles of hiking.
Features you'll appreciate: Trails in the park link up with the Taconite State Trail and offer snowmobilers, skiers, and hikers plenty to enjoy.
Directions: From Tower, take US Highway 169 east nine miles to County Highway 128, then go south seven miles to the park.

Old Mill State Park
33489 240th Avenue NW, Argyle, MN 56713
218-437-8174•www.dnr.state.mn.us/state_parks/old_mill/trails.html

Amenities: One mile of self-guided trail and seven miles of hiking trail.

Features you'll appreciate: Old Mill State Park offers a swimming area, swinging bridge, picnic grounds, campground, and interpretive displays.
Directions: From Argyle, go twelve miles east on County Road 4, then one mile north on County Road 4 to County Road 39.

Lake Bemidji State Park
3401 State Park Road NE, Bemidji, MN 56601
218-308-2300
www.dnr.state.mn.us/state_parks/lake_bemidji/trails.html

Amenities: Fifteen miles of easy to moderate trails. No winter hiking trails. Seven miles paved bike trail that connects with Paul Bunyan State Trail. Five miles of mountain bike trail within the park.
Features you'll appreciate: Two miles of handicapped accessible trail. One mile of self-guided trails, includes boardwalk and Rocky Point trail.
Directions: Ten minutes north of Bemidji off US Highway 71.

Paul Bunyan State Trail
Crow Wing State Park (south of Brainerd/Baxter) to Lake Bemidji State Park (north of Bemidji)
www.paulbunyantrail.com

Amenities: 110 miles of trails connect the Heartland State Trail, the Blue Ox Trail, and the Cuyuna State Trail. Paved from Brainerd to Lake Bemidji State Park. The trail offers biking, hiking, inline skating, and snowmobiling.
Features you'll appreciate: The Paul Bunyan Trail is the longest bike trail in Minnesota and has many areas to stop and rest.
Directions: The southern trailhead is in Baxter at the trail's intersection with Excelsior Road near the junction of Minnesota Highway 371 and Minnesota Highway 210. The trail ends with the junction of the Blue Ox Trail at Lake Bemidji State Park.

Chippewa National Forest
200 Ash Avenue NW, Cass Lake, MN 56633
218-335-8600•www.fs.usda.gov/Chippewa

Amenities: Forty-one miles of paved bike trails on the west side and forty-three miles of unpaved trails for mountain bikers on the east side between Deer River and Marcell.
Features you'll appreciate: The Chippewa National Forest offers more than 290 miles of hiking trails.
Directions: Obtain detailed maps and information from forest headquarters in Cass Lake near the intersection of US Highway 2 and Minnesota Highway 371.

Scenic State Park
56956 Scenic Highway 7, Bigfork, MN 56628
218-743-3362•www.dnr.state.mn.us/state_parks/scenic/trails.html

Amenities: Fourteen miles of easy to moderate hiking trails through wooded areas. Two miles of paved bike trails.
Features you'll appreciate: Two miles of self-guided trails. The Tell Lake and Chase Point trails have interpretive signs.
Directions: Seven miles east of Bigfork on County Road 7.

McCarthy Beach State Park
7622 McCarthy Beach Road, Side Lake, MN 55781
218-254-7979
www.dnr.state.mn.us/state_parks/mccarthy_beach/trails.html

Amenities: Eighteen miles of hiking trails, seventeen miles of mountain bike trails, and sixteen miles of horse trail. Access to the Taconite State Trail.
Features you'll appreciate: The Pickerel Lake trail is the favorite of visitors.

Directions: From Hibbing, take US Highway 169 north to County Road 5, then follow that north fifteen miles to the park.

Grand Portage State Park
9393 E. Minnesota Highway 61, Grand Portage, MN 55605
218-475-2360
www.dnr.state.mn.us/state_parks/grand_portage/trails.html

Amenities: One-half mile accessible boardwalk trail to the overlook area at the High Falls, Minnesota's highest waterfall; four miles of hiking trails.
Features you'll appreciate: Lake Superior is about one mile east of the park.
Directions: From Grand Marais, northeast on Minnesota Highway 61 for thirty-six miles to the US-Canadian border. The park entrance is on the west side of the highway, just before the US Customs Station.

Judge C.R. Magney State Park
4051 E. Minnesota Highway 61, Grand Marais, MN 55604
218-387-3039
www.dnr.state.mn.us/state_parks/judge_cr_magney/trails.html

Amenities: Nine miles of moderate to challenging hiking trail runs along the Brule River to a series of waterfalls, the most famous of which is the Devil's Kettle, where part of the Brule River falls into a huge caldron and never emerges.
Features you'll appreciate: One-mile self-guided nature trail and other trails wind through the forest areas. The Superior Hiking Trail loops through the parking area.
Directions: Fourteen miles northeast of Grand Marais on Minnesota Highway 61.

Cascade River State Park
3481 W. Minnesota Highway 61, Lutsen, MN 55612
218-387-3053
www.dnr.state.mn.us/state_parks/cascade_river/trails.html

Amenities: Eighteen miles of scenic hiking trails.
Features you'll appreciate: The Superior Hiking Trail runs through the park.
Directions: Ten miles southwest of Grand Marais on Minnesota Highway 61.

Temperance River State Park
7620 W. Minnesota Highway 61, Schroeder, MN 55613
218-663-7476
www.dnr.state.mn.us/state_parks/temperance_river/trails.html

Amenities: Twenty-two miles of hiking trails with access to the Superior Hiking Trail; several short, easy spurs down either side of the river to Lake Superior, a catwalk bridge, and trails up both sides of the river and through the adjacent woodlands. Also a half-mile self-guided trail.
Features you'll appreciate: A main trailhead for the Superior Hiking Trail and North Shore Corridor Trail is located in the park.
Directions: Entrance one mile north of Schroeder on Highway 61.

George H. Crosby Manitou State Park
7616 County Road 7, Finland, MN 55603
218-226-6365
www.dnr.state.mn.us/state_parks/george_crosby_manitou/trails.html

Amenities: Twenty-four miles of hiking trails through rugged and scenic back-country trails.

Features you'll appreciate: Five miles of the Superior Hiking Trail runs through the park.

Directions: From Minnesota Highway 61, turn inland at Illgen City on Minnesota Highway 1 to Finland, then go seven miles north on County Road 7.

Gitchi-Gami State Trail
Two Harbors to Grand Marais,
along the North Shore of Lake Superior
www.ggta.org

Amenities: Paved trail segments include 3.5 miles connecting popular Gooseberry Falls State Park to Split Rock Lighthouse State Park. The trail will eventually connect five state parks, several communities, four scientific and natural areas, and numerous historic sites, and provide visuals of Lake Superior.

Features you'll appreciate: When completed, the trail will be an eighty-six-mile nonmotorized, paved trail between Two Harbors and Grand Marais.

Directions: Find parking and trail access along Minnesota Highway 61 at the Silver Creek Wayside West, in Beaver Bay near the Beaver River, at the Tofte Town Park, and in Grand Marais near the US Coast Guard Station.

Split Rock Lighthouse State Park
3755 Split Rock Lighthouse Road, Two Harbors, MN 55616
218-226-6377
www.dnr.state.mn.us/state_parks/Split_rock_lighthouse/trails.html

Amenities: Twelve miles of hiking trail, three miles of which run along the Lake Superior shore. Six miles of mountain bike trail begin at the picnic area and follow the hiking trail.

Features you'll appreciate: A quarter-mile handicapped accessible trail in the picnic area follows the shoreline of Lake Superior.
Directions: Twenty miles northeast of Two Harbors on Minnesota Highway 61.

Gooseberry Falls State Park
3206 E. Minnesota Highway 61, Two Harbors, MN 55616
218-834-3855
www.dnr.state.mn.us/state_parks/gooseberry_falls/trails.html

Amenities: Twenty miles of hiking trails along the Gooseberry River. Fifteen miles of paved bike trails; two-and-a-half miles of the trail connect to the Gitchi-Gami State Trail.
Features you'll appreciate: One mile handicapped accessible trail begins at the visitor center to the main falls center.
Directions: From Two Harbors, thirteen miles northeast on Minnesota Highway 61.

Buffalo River State Park
565 155th Street S., Glyndon, MN 56547
218-498-2124
www.dnr.state.mn.us/state_parks/buffalo_river/trails.html

Amenities: Twelve miles of hiking trail on flat terrain through forest and prairies. One mile of self-guided trail.
Features you'll appreciate: Six miles of winter hiking trail.
Directions: From Moorhead, go fourteen miles east on US Highway 10 and follow the signs to the park.

Itasca State Park
36750 Main Park Drive, Park Rapids, MN 56470
218-699-7251
www.dnr.state.mn.us/state_parks/itasca/trails.html

Amenities: Forty-nine miles of hiking trails. Sixteen miles of paved bike trail, six miles of which is an off-road paved trail.

Features you'll appreciate: One-half mile of handicapped accessible trail, including Headwaters Loop Trail and Doctor Roberts Trail, takes you to the Old Timer's Cabin. Three-quarter-mile self-guided trail.

Directions: South entrance to the park is twenty-three miles north of Park Rapids on US Highway 71. From Bemidji, the east entrance is thirty miles south on Highway 71 and one-tenth mile north on Minnesota Highway 200. The north entrance is twenty miles south of Bagley on Minnesota highways 92 and 200.

Heartland State Trail
Between Park Rapids and Cass Lake
www.dnr.state.mn.us/state_trails/heartland/index.html

Amenities: Forty-nine mile multiple-use trail on a level abandoned railroad grade except for a four-mile segment north of Walker. The twenty-seven mile segment between Park Rapids and Walker is paved and has a grassy treadway for horseback riding and mountain biking. The twenty-mile segment from Walker to Cass Lake is also paved.

Features you'll appreciate: The trail passes through forests and along many lakes and streams.

Directions: The trailheads for the paved section of the Heartland State Trail are in Park Rapids and Walker. Parking is available in Park Rapids at Heartland County Park, in Dorset, Nevis, Akeley, and Walker, and at Erickson's Landing north of Walker.

Willard Munger State Trail
Seventy miles from Hinckley to Duluth
www.dnr.state.mn.us/state_trails/willard_munger/index.html

Amenities: The trail consists of three different segments. The sixty-three mile paved Hinckley–Duluth segment connects Hinckley, Willow River, Moose Lake, Barnum, Carlton, and Duluth. The Alex Laveau Memorial Trail takes riders from Gary-New Duluth sixteen miles through Wrenshall into Carlton. Six miles of off-road paved trail from Carlton to Minnesota Highway 23 are open. The remaining miles are a combination of bike routes on paved highway shoulders. The Matthew Lourey State Trail is an eighty-mile, natural surface trail used primarily for snowmobiling, horseback riding, hiking, and mountain biking. This trail passes through remote forests linking St. Croix State Park with the Chengwatana, St. Croix, and Nemadji state forests.

Features you'll appreciate: The Willard Munger Trail is one of the longest paved trails in the United States.

Directions: The southern trailhead is in Hinckley one block north of the Hinckley Fire Museum and the northern trailhead is at Grand Avenue (Highway 23) and 75th Avenue W. in Duluth, behind the Willard Munger Inn. Parking also available in Finlayson, Willow River, Moose Lake, and Barnum.

Jay Cooke State Park
780 E. Minnesota Highway 210, Carlton, MN 55718
218-384-4610
www.dnr.state.mn.us/state_parks/jay_cooke/trails.html

Amenities: Eight miles of paved bike trails. Inline skates are permitted on the trails. Thirteen miles of mountain bike trails (inquire at park for location information).

Features you'll appreciate: Fifty miles of hiking through wooded areas and along the St. Louis River.

Directions: From Interstate 35, take Exit 235 toward Carlton and go three miles east of Carlton on Highway 210.

Moose Lake State Park
4252 County Road 137, Moose Lake, MN 55767
218-485-5420
www.dnr.state.mn.us/state_parks/moose_lake/trails.html

Amenities: Five miles of easy to moderate hiking trails through forests and meadows, and along marshes and lakes.
Features you'll appreciate: One-third mile paved trail handicapped accessible. The trail begins at the picnic grounds to the handicapped accessible fishing pier.
Directions: From Interstate 35, go a quarter-mile east at Exit 214 and go east on County Road 137 until you see the park signs.

Cuyuna Lakes State Trail
307 Third Street, Ironton, MN 56455
218-546-5926
www.cuyunalakestrail.org

Amenities: More than six miles of paved trail, mostly in the Cuyuna Country State Recreation Area that consists of regenerated vegetation and clear lakes.
Features you'll appreciate: Twenty-two miles of single-track mountain bike trails, including beginner, intermediate, and advanced routes.
Directions: Near the communities of Crosby and Ironton.

Banning State Park
61101 Banning Park Road, Sandstone, MN 55072
320-245-2668
www.dnr.state.mn.us/state_parks/banning/trails.html

Amenities: Seventeen miles of hiking trail and 1.8 miles of self-guided trail.
Features you'll appreciate: Trail connects to the Willard Munger State Trail.
Directions: From Interstate 35, take Exit 195 to Minnesota Highway 23 and take the first right to the park.

St. Croix State Park
30065 St. Croix Park Road, Hinckley, MN 55037
320-384-6591
www.dnr.state.mn.us/state_parks/st_croix/trails.html

Amenities: 127 miles of easy hiking trails. Five-and-a-half miles of paved bike trails and twenty-one miles of mountain bike trails.
Features you'll appreciate: One-and-a-half miles of handicapped accessible and self-guided trail, beginning at the interpretive center.
Directions: From Interstate 35, take Exit 183 at Hinckley and go fifteen miles east on Minnesota Highway 48, then five miles south on County Road 22.

Casinos

Seven Clans Casino
1012 E. Lake Street, Warroad, MN 56763
800-815-8293 or 218-386-3381
www.sevenclanscasino.com/page/wr_history

Amenities: The casino has 13,608 square feet, 500 slot machines, and six blackjack and poker tables. Open twenty-four hours daily.

Features you'll appreciate: The Lake of the Woods area offers fishing, camping, snowmobiling, boating, and historical sites. Other places of interest: Canadian National Depot, Harbor Park, Indian burial grounds, Beltrami Island State Forest, Veterans Memorial, and Warroad Summer Theatre.

Directions: In Warroad, turn east off Minnesota Highway 11 (State Avenue) onto Lake Street and go east eleven blocks.

Seven Clans Casino, Hotel, & Water Park
20595 Center Street E., Thief River Falls, MN 56701
866-255-7848 or 800-881-0712
www.sevenclanscasino.com/page/rtf_amenities

Amenities: More than 750 slot machines, including video poker, video keno, and progressives offering huge jackpots. Blackjack and the Ishkode Poker Room.

Features you'll appreciate: Hotel with 151 suites featuring 40,000 square feet of indoor water park. Open twenty-four hours daily.

Directions: About ten miles southeast of Thief River Falls off US Highway 59 on County Road 3 E. (Center Street E.).

Fortune Bay Resort Casino
1430 Bois Forte Road, Tower, MN 55790
218-753-6400 or 800-992-7529, ext. 1
www.fortunebay.com

Amenities: Blackjack, poker, 750 slot machines, video poker, keno, bingo, restaurant, grill, entertainment, two full-service bars, 174-room resort, conference center, and nationally known The Wilderness at Fortune Bay golf course.

Features you'll appreciate: On the shores of Lake Vermilion for fishing, boating, snowmobiling, and cross-country skiing.

Directions: From US Highway 169 north toward Ely, turn left on Angus Road/County Road 77; turn right at County Road 413/Lake Vermilion Reservation Road; turn left at Gold Mine Spur Road. Take the first left to stay on Gold Mine Spur Road.

Seven Clans Casino, Hotel, and Event Center
10200 Highway 89, Red Lake, MN 56671
888-679-2501 or 218-679-2500
www.sevenclanscasino.com/page/ourhistory

Amenities: A new $21 million complex had its grand opening in 2010, with more than 250 slot machines, blackjack, poker, and video keno, plus a restaurant, event center, and a new forty-room, all-suite hotel.

Features you'll appreciate: There's a wide range of things to do in the Red Lake area, including fishing, camping, golfing, hiking, biking, hunting, and snowmobiling. Visit Itasca State Park, Headwaters Science Center, Bemidji State Park, Camp Rabideau, and Paul Bunyan Animal Land.

Directions: Just east of Highway 89 south of Red Lake, just south of the Red Lake Indian Reservation boundary.

Grand Portage Lodge and Casino
80 Casino Drive, Grand Portage, MN 55605
800-543-1384 or 218-475-2401•www.grandportage.com

Amenities: The 15,000-square-foot casino on the North Shore of Lake Superior contains a bingo hall and more than 450 slot machines, including video slots. There is a ninety-five-room lodge with indoor heated pool, sauna, and three-story fireplace; suites feature fireplaces and Jacuzzis; there are also cabins, marina, and an RV park. The Island View Dining Room features wild rice buttermilk pancakes, fresh local fish, and hearty steaks.

Features you'll appreciate: The Trading Post is a smoke-free facility adjacent to the lodge and casino. Visitors can stop at the gift shop, grab a bite to eat, pick up some groceries, use the UPS parcel pickup, and have fun gaming with forty-three slot machines. Convenient to Grand Portage National Monument and Heritage Center.

Directions: Off Minnesota Highway 61 in Grand Portage, two and a half hours north of Duluth.

Palace Casino and Hotel
16599 69th Avenue NW, Cass Lake, MN 56633
218-335-7000 or 800-228-6676
www.palacecasinohotel.com

Amenities: More than 500 slots, keno, video poker, and wide-area progressive machines. Bingo lovers can choose 20/20 or high-stakes bingo. Live blackjack with tournaments held weekly.

Features you'll appreciate: Alcohol-free environment. Full-service casual dining restaurant and café, hotel with Jacuzzi suites, meeting rooms with catering menu available, and RV parking. Open twenty-four hours daily.

Directions: About fifteen miles southeast of Bemidji on US Highway 2, then north 1.4 miles on 69th Avenue NW.

Shooting Star Casino, Hotel, and Event Center
777 Casino Road, Mahnomen, MN 56557
800-453-7827 or 218-935-2711 • www.starcasino.com

Amenities: Poker room, blackjack, slots, bingo, 390-room hotel, four restaurants, live entertainment lounge, full-service spa, 28,000-square-foot event center, and an RV park.

Features you'll appreciate: Nonsmoking slot area and a private high-stakes room (blackjack and slot machines). The 2 One 8 restaurant features a full menu of fine dining. Open twenty-four hours daily.

Directions: Off US Highway 59 on southeast edge of Mahnomen.

White Oak Casino
45830 US Highway 2, Deer River, MN 56636
800-653-2412
www.whiteoakcasino.com

Amenities: This small casino features 306 slot machines, two black-jack tables, and poker. Opened in 2000, it is the newest of the Leech Lake Band of Ojibwe's three casinos and is named for the White Oak Point Band of Ojibwe, who have lived in the area for centuries.

Features you'll appreciate: A gift shop, snack bar, and full-service bar.

Directions: At the intersection of Highway 2 and Minnesota Highway 46 in Deer River, about fifteen miles northwest of Grand Rapids.

Fond-Du-Luth Casino
129 E. Superior Street, Duluth, MN 55802
800-873-0280 or 218-722-0280•www.fondduluthcasino.com

Amenities: More than 750 video slot machines and four blackjack tables in downtown Duluth.

Features you'll appreciate: Free shuttle to and from Black Bear Casino south of Duluth. Convenient to major Duluth attractions.

Directions: From Interstate 35 north, take Exit 256B (Fifth Avenue W./Lake Avenue) in downtown Duluth; left onto Lake Avenue; one block to E. Superior Street; turn right and go one and a half blocks.

Black Bear Casino Resort
1785 Highway 210, Carlton, MN 55718
218-878-2327 or 888-771-0777
www.blackbearcasinoresort.com

Amenities: More than 2,000 slot machines, poker, blackjack, bingo, and high-limit areas. Three restaurants, hotel with 10,000-square-foot indoor pool complex, a conference center, and eighteen-hole championship golf.

Features you'll appreciate: Entertainment in the Cobalt Nightclub and Cabaret and the Otter Creek Event Center. Free wireless in coffee shop and hotel lobby. Open twenty-four hours daily.

Directions: Off Interstate 35 at the Carlton exit (Exit 235).

Northern Lights Casino, Hotel, & Event Center
6800 Y Frontage Road NW, Walker, MN 56484
218-547-2744 or 800-252-7529•www.northernlightscasino.com

Amenities: More than 900 slot machines including video poker, ten blackjack tables, and poker room. Buffet, restaurant, snack bar, and full-service catering menu in the event center.

Features you'll appreciate: National and regional entertainment; 105-room hotel, which includes Jacuzzi suites, pool, hot tub, sauna, and arcade; 9,000-square-foot event center; gift shop.

Directions: On Minnesota highways 371 and 200 about five miles southeast of Walker and left at Y Frontage Road NW.

Grand Casino Hinckley
777 Lady Luck Drive, Hinckley, MN 55037
320-384-7777 or 800-472-6321
www.grandcasinomn.com

Amenities: More than 2,400 video slots, keno, and poker machines, thirty-two blackjack table games, a poker room, a 312-seat bingo hall, and a large no-smoking area.

Features you'll appreciate: The complex has a 5,000-seat outdoor amphitheater, five restaurants, lounge, 22,480-square-foot convention and events center, hotels, rental chalets, RV resort, child care, spa, video arcade, live entertainment seven days a week, eighteen-hole championship golf course, and liquor.

Directions: From Interstate 35, take Exit 183, turn east on Minnesota Highway 48 (Fire Monument Road), and continue to the casino.

Golf
Courses

Warroad Estates Golf Course
37293 Elm Drive, Warroad, MN 56763
218-386-2025•www.warroadestates.com

Amenities: Eighteen-hole championship course, par 72, 6,942-yard design, clubhouse with full bar, concessions, weekend grill, pro shop, club and electric golf cart rental available.
Features you'll appreciate: Open to the public. Banquet facilities, stay-and-play packages, and large group discounts.
Directions: In Warroad on Minnesota Highway 313 one mile north of the intersection of Highway 313 and Minnesota Highway 11.

Oak Harbor Golf Course
2805 Twenty-Fourth Street NW, Baudette, MN 56623
218-634-9939•www.oakharborgolfcourse.com

Amenities: Eighteen-hole course, open from dawn to dusk, open seven days a week, clubhouse with a restaurant, and cart and equipment rental.
Features you'll appreciate: The course operates from May 1 to October 15 and is open to the public.
Directions: Nine miles north of Baudette on Minnesota Highway 172.

Falls Country Club
4402 County Road 152, International Falls, MN 56649
218-283-4491•www.fallscc.com

Amenities: Open to the public, championship course, par 72, measuring 6,632 yards from the back tees with a course rating/slope of 72.2.
Features you'll appreciate: Practice facility available, pro shop, food and beverage service, and beverage cart is available.
Directions: West of International Falls off US Highway 71 (on Golf Course Road).

Babbitt Golf

Club Highway 21, Babbitt, MN 55706

www.babbitt-mn.com

Amenities: Nine-hole course, 3,208 yards long for nine holes and 5,420 for eighteen holes. Par is 35 for men and 36 for women.

Features you'll appreciate: Public golf course. The clubhouse has kitchen facilities and food available, pro shop with golf supplies, golf cart rental, pull cart rental, and storage for personal golf clubs and pull carts.

Directions: One and one-quarter miles west of Babbitt on County Highway 21.

Gunflint Hills Golf Club

1181 Golf Course Road, Grand Marais, MN 55604

218-387-9988 or 218-387-1712

www.grandmaraisgolfcourse.com

Amenities: Nine-hole course, par 36, 3,030 yards with three sets of tees, known for smooth and fast greens with lush fairways and approach areas.

Features you'll appreciate: Native grasses and wildflower plantings along the course—and you may spot a moose.

Directions: From Minnesota Highway 61 at Grand Marais, turn north on Gunflint Trail for four miles, then turn east on County Road 55 and one block to parking.

Superior National at Lutsen
5731 Minnesota Highway 61, Lutsen, MN 55612
218-663-7195 or 888-564-6543 • www.superiornational.com

Amenities: Twenty-seven holes, par 27, twenty of the twenty-seven holes have views of Lake Superior. Stay-and-play golf packages are available.

Features you'll appreciate: Public course. Voted Minnesota's top "muny" in *Golf Digest*.

Directions: On Highway 61 at Lutsen, ninety miles northeast of Duluth.

Castle Highlands Golf Course
13848 Gull Lake Loop Road NE, Bemidji, MN 56619
218-586-2681 • www.golfcastles.com

Amenities: The Turtle River winds through the course, which also has wetlands, ponds, rolling hills, and wildlife. Eighteen-hole golf course, 6,030 yards, and a par 72.

Features you'll appreciate: A back-nine expansion added nearly 1,000 yards to the course. The course includes a full-shot driving range and an 11,000-square-foot putting green.

Directions: Ten miles north of Bemidji at the intersection of US Highway 71 and County Road 23.

Mahnomen Country Club
2267 155th Avenue, Mahnomen, MN 56557
218-935-5188 • www.mahnomencountryclub.com

Amenities: Nine-hole golf course and driving range, open daily to the public.

Features you'll appreciate: Club house with bar and short-order food available.

Directions: Three-quarters mile east of Mahnomen on County Road 25, then a quarter-mile north to the course.

Ruttger's Sugarbrooke Golf Course
37584 Otis Lane, Cohasset, MN 55721
218-327-1462 or 800-450-4555
www.sugarlakelodge.com

Amenities: Eighteen-hole course, par 71, on 6,534 yards of terrain with woods, water, and bunkers.

Features you'll appreciate: Golf packages available, club and cart rentals. Jack's Bar & Grill overlooks the eighteenth hole, serving lunch and dinner.

Directions: At Ruttger's Sugar Lake Lodge, twelve miles southwest of Grand Rapids.

Eagle Ridge Golf Course
One Green Way, Coleraine, MN 55722
218-245-2217 or 888-307-3245 • http://golfeagleridge.com

Amenities: Eighteen-hole championship course, par 72, practice range, pro shop, and clubhouse with full bar and restaurant.

Features you'll appreciate: The course plays through the woods with views of Trout Lake.

Directions: From US Highway 169 in Coleraine, between Grand Rapids and Hibbing, turn south on McClean Avenue, right on Green Way.

Mesaba Country Club
415 E. Fifty-First Street, Hibbing, MN 55746
218-262-2851 • www.mesabacc.com

Amenities: Eighteen-hole course, par 72, golf instruction is available from a PGA professional, fine dining, lounge, and snack bar. Club and cart rentals, driving range, and practice greens are available.
Features you'll appreciate: Semi-private golf course; public play encouraged.
Directions: About two miles south of Hibbing; follow First Avenue (County Road 57) and turn east on Fifty-First Street (Golf Links Road).

Eveleth Municipal Golf Course
US Highway 53 S., Eveleth, MN 55734
218-744-7558

Amenities: Nine-hole regulation course, par 36, the longest tee is 6,324 yards. The course rating is 70.2 with a slope rating of 124.
Features you'll appreciate: Municipal golf course is open to public guest.
Directions: Three miles south of Eveleth on Highway 53.

Virginia Golf Course
1308 Eighteenth Street N., Virginia, MN 55792
218-748-7530
www.ironrange.org/recreation/golf/virginia/

Amenities: Eighteen-hole course, par 71, 6,228 yards from the longest tees. The course rating is 69.6 and it has a slope rating of 121. Three new hole designs are available, and there is a new driving range.
Features you'll appreciate: Municipal golf course, new log clubhouse, pro shop, and full service restaurant and bar.
Directions: One mile north of Virginia on US Highway 53.

Hoyt Lakes Golf Course
4099 Allen Junction Road, Hoyt Lakes, MN 55750
218-225-2841 or 218-225-2344
www.hoytlakes.com/recreat/golf/golfmain.htm

Amenities: Nine-hole course borders the Superior National Forest, two sets of tee boxes, and new bunkers.
Features you'll appreciate: Snack bar, golf instruction, rental clubs and carts, driving range, practice green, open May to October, tee times available.
Directions: Half-mile east of Hoyt Lakes off the Superior National Forest Scenic Byway.

Silver Bay Golf Course
19 Golf Course Road, Silver Bay, MN 55614
218-226-3111 • www.silverbaygolf.com

Amenities: Nine-hole regulation course, par 36, measures 3,173 from the back tees. Soft spikes only, driving range, power cart rental, pull cart rental, and club rental.

Features you'll appreciate: Memberships available, outside groups and events welcomed, pro shop, and sandwich grill.

Directions: Fifty miles northeast of Duluth on Minnesota Highway 61. Turn into Silver Bay at the stop light on Highway 61 and follow Outer Drive. Take the first left after Horn Boulevard and an immediate right back onto Outer Drive. Follow Outer Drive one block to Golf Course Road. Turn left onto Golf Course Road and proceed two miles to the clubhouse.

Wendigo Golf Course
20108 Golf Crest Road, Grand Rapids, MN 55744
218-327-2211 or 866-727-7345, ext. 440 • www.wendigolodge.com

Amenities: Eighteen-hole course, 6,756 yards, par 72. The course rating is 72.0 with a slope rating of 132. It features dramatic elevation changes, water hazards, a practice putting green, and a driving range.

Features you'll appreciate: Open to the public. Group tournaments available, lodging, conference facilities, dining, and pro shop available onsite.

Directions: Southeast of Grand Rapids.

Wedgewood Golf Course
6542 Wedgewood Road NW, Walker, MN 56484
218-547-2666

Amenities: Nine-hole course, par 28, 1,535 yards, rental clubs and carts, and a snack bar.

Features you'll appreciate: Public course. The signature hole is number one: 325 yards, par 4, with a dogleg right fairway.

Directions: Five miles north of Walker.

Tianna Country Club
7470 Minnesota Highway 34 NW, Walker, MN 56484
218-547-1712 or 866-482-2465•www.tianna.com

Amenities: Eighteen-hole course, par 72, 6,323 yards, leagues and tournaments available.
Features you'll appreciate: Open to the public, banquet and conference facility, pro shop, and golf lessons.
Directions: From Minnesota highways 371 and 200 in Walker, turn south on Highway 34 (Eighth Street) and go 1.75 miles; Tianna Country Club is on your left.

Ironman Golf Course
20664 County Highway 21, Detroit Lakes, MN 56501
218-847-5592•www.ironmangolf.com

Amenities: Nine holes, par 3, eighteen-hole putting course, lessons, rental equipment, full-size driving range, practice green, and golf cart rentals.
Features you'll appreciate: Clubhouse, lockers, snack bar, and pro shop.
Directions: Three miles north of Detroit Lakes on Richwood Road.

Forest Hills Golf & RV Resort
22931 185th Street, Detroit Lakes, MN 56501
218-439-6033 or 800-482-3441•www.foresthillsgolfrv.com

Amenities: Eighteen-hole championship golf course, ranging from 5,008 to 6,346 yards in length, offering three sets of tees.
Features you'll appreciate: New fifteenth hole. They have also completed work on the number two, number sixteen, and number seventeen holes.

Directions: Three and one-half miles west of Detroit Lakes on the south side of US Highway 10.

Detroit Country Club
24591 County Highway 22, Detroit Lakes, MN 56502
218-847-5790 or 218-847-8942•www.detroitcountryclub.com

Amenities: Thirty-six-hole golf, par 71 Pine to Palm course and par 64 Lakeview course. The two courses are bordered by Lake Sallie to the north and Lake Melissa to the south.
Features you'll appreciate: Open to the public.
Directions: Five miles south of Detroit Lakes on US Highway 59.

Lakeview National Golf Course
1349 Minnesota Highway 61 N., Two Harbors, MN 55616
218-834-2664 or 218-830-1009•www.lakeviewnational.com

Amenities: Eighteen-hole championship golf course, bar and grill, and men's and women's leagues.
Features you'll appreciate: Views of Lake Superior from fourteen of the eighteen fairways and tees; large tees and greens.
Directions: Twenty-two miles northeast of Duluth on Highway 61.

Brookside Resort — Golf Course
31671 County Highway 50, Park Rapids, MN 56470
218-732-4093 or 800-247-1615
www.brookside-resort.com/golftenn.html

Amenities: Nine holes of par 3 golf; par is 27 with the course record of 24.
Features you'll appreciate: Clubs and pull cart rental, free golf weeks for registered guests are the first four and last two weeks of their season.

Directions: Eleven miles north of Park Rapids on US Highway 71, west on County Highway 41 and south on County Highway 50. Four hours from the Twin Cities area and one-and-a-half hours from the Fargo-Moorhead area.

Eagleview Golf Course
24988 US Highway 71, Park Rapids, MN 56470
218-732-7102

Amenities: Eighteen-hole executive golf course, 3,617 yards of golf from the longest tees for a par of 64.

Features you'll appreciate: The course rating is 59 and it has a slope rating of 87.

Directions: About eight miles north of Park Rapids on Highway 71.

Evergreen Lodge Golf
17838 Goldeneye Lane, Park Rapids, MN 56470
218-732-4766

Amenities: Nine holes, 1,300 yards, and a public course.

Features you'll appreciate: Rental clubs and pull carts available. No tee times.

Directions: Two miles east and five miles north of Park Rapids on County Road 4 on Big Sand Lake.

Lester Park Golf Course
1860 Lester River Road, Duluth, MN 55804
218-525-0830•http://lesterpark.golfinduluth.com

Amenities: Public course, par 72, twenty-seven holes, views of Lake Superior on twenty holes, driving range, short game area, and fully stocked snack bar.

Features you'll appreciate: PGA golf professionals for individual and group golf lessons, leagues and tournaments available, season passes, twilight golf, club rental, and golf cart rental.

Directions: From Interstate 35, continue on London Road (Minnesota Highway 61 along Lake Superior) to Sixty-First Avenue E. (Lester River Road), go left uphill, golf course on right.

Black Bear Golf Course

1791 Minnesota Highway 210, Carlton, MN 55718

218-878-2483 or 888-771-0777 • www.golfatthebear.com

Amenities: Eighteen-hole championship course, par 72, driving range, two practice greens, and a GPS system on all electric golf carts.

Features you'll appreciate: A pro shop and a full-service snack bar. They have fly-over videos of every hole on the course.

Directions: From Interstate 35 twenty miles south of Duluth, exit to Highway 210 (Exit 235) at Carlton. Course is adjacent to the Black Bear Casino Resort.

Sandstone Area Country Club

343 Lark Street, Sandstone, MN 55072

320-245-0471

Amenities: Eighteen-hole course features 2,581 yards of golf from the longest tees for a par of 35.

Features you'll appreciate: The course rating is 32.7 and it has a slope rating of 115.

Directions: From Interstate 35, take the Sandstone exit (Exit 191) and go east for two miles, left at stop sign.

Grand National Golf Club
300 Lady Luck Drive, Hinckley, MN 55037
320-384-7427•www.grandnationalgolf.com

Amenities: Eighteen-hole championship course, 6,900 yards of fairways, pro shop, golf lessons, outings and tournaments hosted, memberships, golf leagues, play-and-stay packages, and golf leagues.
Features you'll appreciate: Next to Grand Casino Hinckley, offering five restaurants, two lounges, and more than 700 hotel rooms.
Directions: From Interstate 35 midway between Minneapolis-St. Paul and Duluth, take the Hinckley exit (Exit 183) and go east.

Pine City Country Club
10413 Golf Course Road SW, Pine City, MN 55063
320-629-3848

Amenities: Nine-hole regulation course, 3,240 yards of golf from the longest tees for a par of 36, course rating is 35.2 with a slope rating of 119.
Features you'll appreciate: Public course, daily fee golf course, and a call for privileges guest policy.
Directions: Located one-half mile southwest of Pine City on Golf Course Road.

Shopping

WARROAD

Dollar Savers
210 Main Avenue, Warroad, MN 56763
218-386-1247

What you'll find: Discount dollar store offering scrapbooking items, party supplies, greeting cards, food, and seasonal items.

Heritage Health-Mart and Jewelry
321 Lake Street NE, Warroad, MN 56763
218-386-1088

What you'll find: Gifts, jewelry, health and beauty supplies, full-service pharmacy, and ice cream soda fountain.

North Country Convenience
34480 550th Avenue, Warroad, MN 56763
218-386-2726 • www.northcountryfudgeshoppe.com

What you'll find: Homemade fudge in the North Country Fudge Shoppe, live bait, information on fishing hotspots, convenience items, gas, and propane. Full deli, pizza, homemade butter-cream fudge, and old-fashioned ice cream.

Northern Exposure Quilts
210 Main Avenue NE, Suite B, Warroad, MN 56763
218-386-4809 • www.nequilts.com

What you'll find: Classes for all levels of quilters from beginner to expert, fabric, patterns, notions, and thread.

Rhoda's Closet

106 Wabasha Avenue NE, Warroad, MN 56763
218-386-1214

What you'll find: Hockeytown USA sweatshirts, T-shirts, jeans, jewelry, sportswear, accessories, and purses.

Soulutions Hobby, Home & Heart

112 Main Avenue NE, Warroad, MN 56763
218-386-1720•www.soulutionstore.com

What you'll find: Quilting items, fabric, Christian bookstore, scrapbooking items, frames, Office Depot outlet, toys, kids' crafts, party favors, fish, birds, pets, beads, Over Coffee Espresso Café, and mini golf.

Streiff Sporting Goods

34480 550th Avenue, Warroad, MN 56763
218-386-2590 or 800-817-2590•www.streiffs.com

What you'll find: Camping gear, hunting equipment, guns and gun supplies, fishing equipment, hockey equipment and apparel, casual clothing, footwear, trophy mounts throughout the store, kids' club, and indoor archery range.

T-Shirt Barrel

116 Lake Street NE, Warroad, MN 56763
218-386-2728•www.tshirtbarrel.com

What you'll find: Commercial embroidery and screen printing on all apparel and accessories.

Thomson's Thrifty White Drug
408 Lake Street NE, Warroad, MN 56763
218-386-2453 • www.thomsondrug.com

What you'll find: Full-service pharmacy, gifts and jewelry, one-hour photo developing, and greeting cards.

Trading Post Gift Shop
1109 McKenzie Street, Warroad, MN 56763
218-386-1440

What you'll find: Gifts, jewelry, T-shirts, sweatshirts, kids' clothing, moccasins, candles, purses, souvenirs, kids' treats, candy, old-fashioned hard ice cream, wild rice, lake maps, gourmet foods, Minnesota items, greeting cards, and garden flags.

INTERNATIONAL FALLS

Alli-Kat Floral & Embroidery
328 Third Street, International Falls, MN 56649
218-283-6779

What you'll find: Floral creations and embroidery services.

The Bootery
316 Third Street, International Falls, MN 56649
218-283-8381

What you'll find: Shoes and boots for men and women.

Border Bobs
200 Second Avenue, International Falls, MN 56649
218-283-4414•www.borderbobs.com

What you'll find: Ice cream shop, sports apparel, souvenirs, art gallery, books, jewelry, and homemade fudge.

Borderland Jewelry
324 Third Street, International Falls, MN 56649
218-283-4701

What you'll find: Jewelry.

Dollar Tree Stores
1905 Valley Pine Circle, International Falls, MN 56649
218-283-0864

What you'll find: Vases, toys, school supplies, snacks, and sanitizers; pet, party, and office supplies; household and health supplies; games, floral creations, electronics, dinnerware, and craft items.

Iverne's
309 Third Street, Suite 1, International Falls, MN 56649
218-283-9246

What you'll find: Clothes, jewelry, and swimsuits.

The Loon's Nest
415 Minnesota Highway 11 E., International Falls, MN 56649
218-286-5850

What you'll find: Convenience store, groceries, gas, bait, and tackle.

Quilter's Corner
309 Third Street, Suite 10, International Falls, MN 56649
218-285-2080 • www.quilterscorner-mn.com

What you'll find: Quilting and quilting supplies.

Ronnings
301 Third Street, International Falls, MN 56649
218-283-8877 • www.ronnings.com

What you'll find: Clothes, books, shoes, gifts, and souvenirs.

THIEF RIVER FALLS

Annie's Attic
321 Main Avenue N., Thief River Falls, MN 56701
218-681-6648

What you'll find: Used furniture, toys, silver, pottery, kerosene lanterns, farm tools, English china, Depression glass, artwork, antiques, and collectibles.

Diamonds & Designs
207 Labree Avenue N., Thief River Falls, MN 56701
888-834-2436

What you'll find: Jewelry and gifts.

Hunters Outlet
206 Knight Avenue N., Thief River Falls, MN 56701
218-681-3030•www.huntersoutletinc.com

What you'll find: Tree stands and blinds; firearms, optics, muzzle-loading equipment, hunting apparel and accessories; archery, ammo, gun safes, decoys, cross bows, and archery accessories.

Keen Looks
117 Third Street E., Thief River Falls, MN 56701
218-684-5411

What you'll find: Thrift shop and spray tanning.

Legends Sporting Goods and Susy's Sewing Corner
1845 US Highway 59 S., Thief River Falls, MN 56701
218-681-1006•www.susyssewingcorner.com

What you'll find: Sporting goods, fabrics, notions, and apparel.

Maurices
1775 US Highway 59 S., Thief River Falls, MN 56701
218-681-7343

What you'll find: Women's apparel.

Northern Gun & Pawn
311 Main Avenue N., Thief River Falls, MN 56701
218-681-6611

What you'll find: Guns, sporting goods, and pawn shop.

Northern Lights Books & Crafts
208 Labree Avenue N., Thief River Falls, MN 56701
218-681-8242

What you'll find: Secondhand store with used books, clothing, and miscellaneous items.

Purdy's Shoe Store
209 Labree Avenue N., Thief River Falls, MN 56701
218-681-2608

What you'll find: Shoes, scarves, socks, long underwear, clothing, and suits.

The Specialty Corner
14914 158th Street NE, Thief River Falls, MN 56701
218-681-7204

What you'll find: Gifts and decorations for all occasions.

The Shed

17526 Minnesota Highway 1 NE, Thief River Falls, MN 56701
218-681-4261

What you'll find: Antiques.

EAST GRAND FORKS

Glamorous Re-Runs Consignment Boutique

402 Third Street NW, East Grand Forks, MN 56721
218-399-0154

What you'll find: Clothes, luggage, purses, shoes, and jewelry.

Knick Knack Paddy Whacks Card and Gift

211 Demers Avenue, East Grand Forks, MN 56721
218-773-5616

What you'll find: Cards and gifts.

Quilter's Eden

223 Demers Avenue, East Grand Forks, MN 56721
218-773-0773 • www.quilterseden.com

What you'll find: Fabrics, notions, kits, books, patterns, long arm quilting services, and Janome machines.

T N T Outfitters
211 Demers Avenue, East Grand Forks, MN 56721
218-773-8683

What you'll find: Men's clothes, work boots, casual shoes, and work clothing.

CROOKSTON

Crookston Floral & Antiques
115 N. Broadway, Crookston, MN 56716
218-281-3549•www.estatesaleguys.com

What you'll find: Retail florist shop, scrapbooking store, art gallery, and antique gallery.

Erickson Embroidery
124 W. Second Street, Crookston, MN 56716
218-281-2801

What you'll find: Embroidery, screen printing, and sporting equipment.

Four Seasons Clothing
101 N. Broadway, Crookston, MN 56716
218-281-5049

What you'll find: Clothes and shoes.

Krazy Kiln

113 S. Broadway, Crookston, MN 56716
218-470-0700 • www.krazykiln.com

What you'll find: Wheel-thrown pottery; quilt shop; wedding registry; personalized gifts for weddings, graduations, and birthdays; and art gallery.

Munn's Jewelers Inc.

109 N. Broadway, Crookston, MN 56716
218-281-3408

What you'll find: Glassware, crystal, gifts, and jewelry.

Spin Magic

115 N. Broadway, Crookston, MN 56716
218-289-4831

What you'll find: Spin art T-shirts, Frisbees, pillow cases, art cards, and aprons.

Willow & Ivy Gift Shop

123 S. Broadway, Crookston, MN 56716
218-281-3104

What you'll find: Gifts and antiques.

Wish Upon A Star

101 S. Broadway, Crookston, MN 56716
218-281-1700

What you'll find: Consignment clothing for all ages and sizes.

GRAND PORTAGE

Grand Portage Trading Post
77 Mile Creek Road, Grand Portage, MN 55605
218-475-2282•www.grandportage.com/tradingpost.php

What you'll find: Convenience store with deli, coffee, gas, slot machines, and gifts.

Ryden's Border Store & 66
9301 Ryden Road, Grand Portage, MN 55605
218-475-2330•www.rydens.com

What you'll find: Parcel service, duty-free store, gas station, café, souvenirs, convenience items, and clothing.

GRAND MARAIS

The Attic Gift Shop
19 W. Wisconsin Street, Grand Marais, MN 55604
218-387-1323

What you'll find: Artwork and gifts by American and Canadian artists.

Bear Track Outfitting Co.
2011 W. Minnesota Highway 61, Grand Marais, MN 55604
218-387-1162•www.bear-track.com

What you'll find: Camping equipment, sporting goods, maps, books, clothing, food, gifts, and fly-fishing supplies.

Betsy Bowen Studio
301 First Avenue W., Grand Marais, MN 55604
218-387-1992•http://woodcut.com

What you'll find: Original woodblock prints made at this local studio, along with cards, calendars, and prints; pottery; jewelry; sculpture; and paintings.

Birchbark Books & Gifts
11 First Avenue W., Grand Marais, MN 55604
218-387-2315

What you'll find: Bookstore, Lego area for children, cabin accessories, clothes, and gifts.

Cabin Antiques & Otherwiz
3 Seventh Avenue W., Grand Marais, MN 55604
218-387-1095

What you'll find: Primitives, fishing items, vintage clothes, glassware, and more.

Crystal's Log Cabin Quilts
1100 W. Minnesota Highway 61, Grand Marais, MN 55604
218-387-3177

What you'll find: Handcrafted quilts for sale, full-service quilt shop, and classes.

Drury Lane Books

12 E. Wisconsin Street, Grand Marais, MN 55604
218-387-3370 • www.drurylanebooks.com

What you'll find: Books.

Eight Broadway Gallery

8 N. Broadway Avenue, Grand Marais, MN 55604
218-387-2044

What you'll find: Oils, watercolors, and carvings by local artists.

The Garage

16 First Avenue W., Grand Marais, MN 55604
218-387-1004

What you'll find: Art, antiques, and collectibles; locally made arts and crafts; coffee and cookies, and Wi-Fi.

Gunflint Mercantile

12 First Avenue W., Grand Marais, MN 55604
218-387-9228 • www.gunflintmercantile.com

What you'll find: Homemade candy, fudge, clothing, ice cream, locally made gifts, coffee, rice, and beans.

Johnson Heritage Post Gallery

115 W. Wisconsin Street, Grand Marais, MN 55604
218-387-2314 • www.cookcountyhistory.org

What you'll find: Items by local artisans.

Lake Superior Trading Post
10 S. First Avenue W., Grand Marais, MN 55604
218-387-2020•www.lstp.com

What you'll find: Gifts, clothes, camping gear, maps, footwear, jewelry, books, and specialty food items.

The Shirt Outfitters
10 First Avenue W., Grand Marais, MN 55604
218-387-2391

What you'll find: T-shirts, sweatshirts with local themes, and screen printing.

Sivertson Gallery
14 W. Wisconsin Street, Grand Marais, MN 55604
218-387-2491•www.sivertson.com

What you'll find: Regional, Canadian, and Alaskan artists.

Stone Harbor Wilderness Supply
20 E. First Street, Grand Marais, MN 55604
218-387-3136•www.stoneharborws.com

What you'll find: Canoes, kayaks, camping and fishing gear; clothing; rentals and tours; and skis and snowshoes.

Superior Design Jewelry
107 W. Wisconsin Street, Grand Marais, MN 55604
218-387-1752•www.stephanhoglund.com

What you'll find: Lake Superior gemstone jewelry.

That Little Red House
113 First Avenue W., Grand Marais, MN 55604
218-387-1094

What you'll find: Yarn, knitting supplies, and patterns.

Threads
16 First Avenue W., Grand Marais, MN 55604
218-387-2691

What you'll find: Clothes at 50 percent off every item, every day.

TLC
4 Eighth Avenue W., Grand Marais, MN 55604
218-387-1943

What you'll find: Antiques and collectibles.

White Pine North
15 W. Wisconsin Street, Grand Marais, MN 55604
218-387-1695

What you'll find: North Woods gifts, sports clothes, coffee, and food.

LUTSEN

Caribou Highlands Lodge Gift Shop
371 Ski Hill Road, Lutsen, MN 55612
800-642-6036 or 218-663-7241•www.caribouhighlands.com

What you'll find: Gifts, apparel for all ages, kids' toys and games, and sundries.

Clearview General Store
5323 W. Minnesota Highway 61, Lutsen, MN 55612
218-663-7478

What you'll find: Groceries, gas, videos, and convenience items.

Great Gifts & Heavy Duty Sewing
5325 W. Minnesota Highway 61, Lutsen, MN 55612
218-663-7669

What you'll find: Toys, cards, jewelry, gifts, purses, packs, and bags made by Heavy Duty Sewing.

Last Chance Fabrication
17 Railroad Drive, Lutsen, MN 55612
218-663-7008•www.lastchancefab.com

What you'll find: Metal art; cast bronze sculpture; architectural metal; cast bronze sinks to original garden sculptures; custom tables to fabricated light fixtures; local and regional artists featured.

Lutsen Resort Gift Shop
5700 W. Minnesota Highway 61, Lutsen, MN 55612
877-881-2907 or 218-663-7212•www.lutsenresort.com

What you'll find: Clothes, gifts, jams, soaps, jewelry, glasses, and other items that evoke the North Shore of Lake Superior.

Mountain Shop at Lutsen Mountains
452 Ski Hill Road, Lutsen, MN 55612
218-663-7842

What you'll find: Clothes for the slopes, books, and gifts.

Solbakken Resort Gift and Bookshop
4874 W. Minnesota Highway 61, Lutsen, MN 55612
218-663-7566•www.solbakkenresort.com

What you'll find: Books, cards, clothes, and gifts.

TOFTE

Bayside Gifts at Bluefin Bay
7192 W. Minnesota Highway 61, Tofte, MN 55615
218-663-7296•www.bluefinbay.com

What you'll find: Sweatshirts, gifts, and souvenirs.

Sawtooth Outfitters
7213 W. Minnesota Highway 61, Tofte, MN 55615
218-663-7643 • www.sawtoothoutfitters.com

What you'll find: Canoe, kayak, and bike rentals; guided canoe and kayak tours; outdoor gear; and bike and ski shop.

Tall Tale Yarn Shop
7197 Bayview Drive, Tofte, MN 55615
218-663-7557 • www.talltaleshop.com

What you'll find: Handmade baskets, hand-knit sweaters, other knit items, and kits.

Waters Edge Trading Company
7124 W. Minnesota Highway 61, Tofte, MN 55615
218-663-7021 • www.watersedgetrading.com

What you'll find: Clothes, gifts, outerwear, clothing, toys, books, cards, jewelry, regional foods, and necessities for camping and hiking.

SILVER BAY

Bri-Esa's Convenience Store
94 Outer Drive, Silver Bay, MN 55614
218-226-4694

What you'll find: Food and convenience items.

Eagles Nest Gifts
6476 Minnesota Highway 61, Silver Bay, MN 55614
218-226-3447

What you'll find: Gifts, gift wrap, cards, and stationery.

Fish Out of Water
6146 Minnesota Highway 61, Silver Bay, MN 55614
218-226-3680

What you'll find: Gifts and souvenirs.

Silver Bay Spur Gifts
44 Outer Drive, Silver Bay, MN 55614
218-226-7220

What you'll find: Fresh flowers and souvenirs.

TWO HARBORS

Agate City Rocks and Gifts
721 Seventh Avenue, Two Harbors, MN 55616
218-834-2304•www.agatecity.com

What you'll find: Lake Superior agates, along with other rocks and minerals; jewelry and locally made jewelry; rock equipment; and gifts.

Anderson's Greenhouse & Florist
1403 Seventh Avenue, Two Harbors, MN 55616
218-834-4837

What you'll find: Floral items and greenhouse.

Buddy's Mercantile
720 Seventh Avenue, Two Harbors, MN 55616
218-834-3303 • www.buddysmercantile.com

What you'll find: Wild rice, jelly, jams, soup mixes; natural, locally produced maple syrup and honey; pancake mixes, homemade soaps, and dry packaged foods; coffee; Watkins products; nostalgic candy; old-fashioned toys; local art, and quilts.

Northwoods Pioneer Gallery & Gifts
2821 Minnesota Highway 61, Two Harbors, MN 55616
218-834-4175 • www.pioneercrafts.com

What you'll find: Handmade items of more than seventy Northland artists and crafters.

The Oldest Sister
830 Seventh Avenue, Two Harbors, MN 55616
218-834-2909

What you'll find: Gifts, books, cards, jewelry, clothes, and kitchen items.

Waterfront Gallery
632 First Avenue, Two Harbors, MN 55616
218-834-0756 • www.waterfront-gallery.com

What you'll find: Fine art, gifts, custom framing, and photo restoration services.

Weldon's Gifts
1065 Minnesota Highway 61 E., Two Harbors, MN 55616
218-834-3462 • www.weldonsgifts.com

What you'll find: Souvenirs, T-shirts, jackets, sweatshirts, moccasins, jewelry, embroidered shirts, and sandals.

KNIFE RIVER

Playing With Yarn
276 Scenic Highway 61, Knife River, MN 55609
218-834-5967 or 877-693-2221 • www.playingwithyarn.com

What you'll find: Yarns, fibers, buttons, Scandinavian gifts, spinning and weaving supplies, and classes.

DULUTH

Art Dock
394 Lake Avenue S., Duluth, MN 55802
218-722-1451

What you'll find: Work by regional artists.

Bagley & Co. Jewelers, China & Gifts
315 W. Superior Street, Duluth, MN 55802
218-727-2991 or 888-829-4661 • www.bagleyandcompany.com

What you'll find: Diamonds, jewelry, china, watches, and giftware.

Blue Heron Trading Co.
394 Lake Avenue S., Duluth, MN 55802
218-722-8799 • www.theblueherontradingcompany.com

What you'll find: Gadgets, gifts, cooking gear, and regional and imported specialty foods.

Blue Lake Gallery
395 Lake Avenue S., Duluth, MN 55802
218-725-0034 • www.bluelakegallery.com

What you'll find: Local and regional artists, pottery, jewelry, metal sculptures, outdoor sculpture garden, handcrafted woodwork, and furniture.

Cookie Temptations
4025 Woodland Avenue, Duluth, MN 55803
218-724-2000 or 877-724-2088 • www.cookietemptations.com

What you'll find: Gourmet sugar cookies that are decorated in fine chocolate.

DeWitt-Seitz Marketplace (Canal Park)
394 Lake Avenue S., Duluth, MN 55802
218-722-0047 • www.dewittseitz.com

What you'll find: Twelve shops, two restaurants, and a bakery.

Duluth Pack Store
365 Canal Park Drive, Duluth, MN 55802
218-722-1707 or 800-849-4489 • www.duluthpack.com

What you'll find: Outdoor clothes and gear, Duluth-made luggage and packs, unique North Woods gifts, and unique book titles of the North.

Fitger's
600 E. Superior Street, Duluth, MN 55802
218-722-8826 • www.fitgers.com

What you'll find: Shops, restaurants, courtyard activities, and museum.

Great Lake Design
4008 Schultz Road, Duluth, MN 55803
218-625-3035 • www.greatlakedesign.com

What you'll find: Gift line highlighting regional landmarks and lighthouses; and graphic design, logo design and illustration for print production and the web.

Harley-Davidson Sport Center, Inc.
4355 Stebner Road, Duluth, MN 55811
218-729-9600 or 888-729-9600•www.hdduluth.com

What you'll find: Harley-Davidson and Buell motorcycles, gifts, leather apparel, parts, and accessories.

Harley-Davidson Sport Center, Inc. Canal Park
345 Lake Avenue S., Duluth, MN 55802
218-625-1146 or 888-729-9600•www.hdduluth.com

What you'll find: Harley-Davidson apparel and gifts.

Hepzibah's Sweet Shoppe
394 Lake Avenue S., Duluth, MN 55802
218-722-5049

What you'll find: Candy, chocolate ore boats, truffles, and imported confections.

Holiday Center
207 W. Superior Street, Duluth, MN 55802
218-727-7765•www.firstpropertiesduluth.com

What you'll find: Forty shops and restaurants.

I Love Duluth
345 Canal Park Drive, Duluth, MN 55802
218-625-1036

What you'll find: Gifts, novelty items, and souvenirs.

Miller Hill Mall
1600 Miller Trunk Highway, Duluth, MN 55811
218-727-8301 • www.miller-hill-mall.com

What you'll find: More than 100 shops and ten food court vendors.

Minnesota Gifts by Sandra Dee
394 Lake Avenue S., Duluth, MN 55802
218-722-3746 • www.minnesotagiftsduluth.com

What you'll find: Clothes, décor, gifts, and souvenirs of Duluth and Minnesota.

Northern Prints Gallery
318 N. Fourteenth Avenue E., Duluth, MN 55805
218-724-3089 • www.northernprintsgallery.com

What you'll find: Hand-printed woodcuts, etchings, screen prints, and other fine art.

Peterson Anderson Flowers
309 W. Superior Street, Duluth, MN 55802
218-722-0888 or 800-569-8133 • www.petersonanderson.com

What you'll find: Flowers, plants, gifts, and balloons.

Rocky Mountain Chocolate Factory
395 Lake Avenue S., Duluth, MN 55802
218-722-1700 • www.rmcf.com/mn/duluth/50533

What you'll find: Fudge, caramel apples, forty varieties of gourmet chocolates, gift baskets, and party trays.

Sivertson Gallery
361 Canal Park Drive, Duluth, MN 55802
218-723-7877 or 888- 815-5814•www.sivertson.com

What you'll find: Original art from the Lake Superior region, jewelry, custom framing, gifts, and Troll beads.

Skylark Company
394 Lake Avenue S., Duluth, MN 55802
218-722-3794

What you'll find: Toys, games puzzles, kites, stuffed animals, rubber stamps, and gifts.

The Snow Goose
600 E. Superior Street, Duluth, MN 55802
218-726-0927

What you'll find: Gifts, jewelry, personal care products, and clothes.

Waters of Superior
395 Lake Avenue S., Duluth, MN 55802
218-786-0233•www.watersofsuperior.com

What you'll find: Clothes, handmade jewelry, regional fine arts, books, and Blacklock photography gallery.

Western Duluth Shopping District
Off Interstate 35 at Central Avenue Exit, Duluth
218-393-6243•www.westduluthmn.com

What you'll find: Variety of shopping, dining, entertainment, and services.

Wood Magic
5105 Miller Trunk Highway, Duluth, MN 55811
218-729-7175 • www.woodmagiconline.com

What you'll find: Gifts and collectibles.

Yarn Harbor
103 Mount Royal Shopping Circle, Duluth, MN 55803
218-724-6432 • www.yarnharborduluth.com

What you'll find: Knitting, crocheting, and felting supplies, and classes.

BEMIDJI

Bad Cat Creations
315 Irvine Avenue NW, Bemidji, MN 56601
218-444-9225 • www.badcatcreations.com

What you'll find: Local art, crafts, gifts, and accessories.

Gallery North
502 Third Street NW, Bemidji, MN 56601
218-444-9813 • www.gallerynorthbemidji.com

What you'll find: Paintings, baskets, fine jewelry, handmade rugs, books, and original wood carvings.

Grandma's Attic Antique Mall
502 Third Street NW, Bemidji, MN 56601
218-759-8931

What you'll find: Antiques and gifts.

Herington's Shoe Store
321 Beltrami Avenue NW, Bemidji, MN 56601
218-751-3736

What you'll find: Shoes, purses, and socks.,

Kat's Book Nook
750 Paul Bunyan Drive NW, Bemidji, MN 56601
218-497-1011

What you'll find: Used books.

Kelsey's As You Like It
318 Beltrami Avenue NW, Bemidji, MN 56601
218-444-4367•www.kelseysjewelry.net

What you'll find: Original jewelry.

Patterson's
200 Third Street NW, Bemidji, MN 56601
218-751-4743

What you'll find: Men's clothing.

TK'z Clozet
217 Third Street NW, Bemidji, MN 56601
218-444-8406•www.tkzclozet.com

What you'll find: Women's, men's, and children's clothing store.

Up North Sports
1900 Division Street W., Suite 7, Bemidji, MN 56601
218-335-8500•www.upnorthsports.com

What you'll find: Snowmobile gear.

Yellow Umbrella
422 Fourth Street SE, Bemidji MN 56601
218-333-6962•www.yellowumbrellashop.com

What you'll find: Handmade screen-printed T-shirts, pottery, jewelry, art, soaps, and lotions.

HIBBING

Bender's Shoe & Sport
405 E. Howard Street, Hibbing MN 55746
218-263-5023•www.bendersshoes.com

What you'll find: Shoes and clothes.

Hibbing Short Stop
2202 First Avenue, Hibbing MN 55746
218-262-4671

What you'll find: Convenience store.

Howard Street Booksellers
115 E. Howard Street, Hibbing, MN 55746
218-262-5206

What you'll find: Used and new books.

Peebles
990 Forty-First Street W., Hibbing, MN 55746
218-263-8377 • www.peebles.com

What you'll find: Women's, men's and children's clothes.

T-Shirt Factory & Odd Shop
406 E. Howard Street, Hibbing, MN 55746
218-262-4224

What you'll find: Screen printing, gifts, cards, T-shirts, apparel, hats, and souvenirs.

GRAND RAPIDS

ABC's of Quilting
Old Central School, 10 NW Fifth Street, Grand Rapids, MN 55744
218-326-9661 • www.abcsofquilting.com

What you'll find: Fabric, kits, patterns, and notions.

Brier's Clothing & Shoes
413 NW First Avenue, Grand Rapids, MN 55744
218-326-2553

What you'll find: Men's clothing store.

Grand Organic Food Market
204 NW First Avenue, No. 8, Grand Rapids, MN 55744
218-326-3663

What you'll find: Organic food.

Hopperton's Moccasin & Gift
401 NW First Avenue, Grand Rapids, MN 55744
218-326-2796

What you'll find: Moccasins, gifts, kids' toys, games, clothes, jewelry, flags, and souvenirs.

Purple Pinecone & Isabella's
201 NW Fourth Street, Grand Rapids, MN 55744
218-327-8119 • www.purplepinecone.com

What you'll find: Wildlife and western art, gifts, home accessories, furniture, clocks, frames, wall borders, candles, gourmet food items, jewelry, and vacation apparel.

Shaw Florists Gifts & Antiques
2 NE Third Street, Grand Rapids, MN 55744
218-326-7429 • www.shawflorists.com

What you'll find: Flowers, plants, gifts, antique furniture, and Amish furniture.

Something Original Art

28 NW Fourth Street, Grand Rapids, MN 55744
218-999-5432

What you'll find: Local artists, jewelry, pottery, sculptures, and paintings.

Terra Reflections

2040 S. Pokegama Avenue, Grand Rapids, MN 55744
218-327-1888 • www.terrareflections.com

What you'll find: Beading supplies, Native American handmade items, jewelry, candles, crystals and gem stones, figurines, and fossils.

Three Bears Candy Company

4 NE Third Street, Grand Rapids, MN 55744
218-327-9933
www.visitgrandrapids.com/shopping/three-bears-candy.html

What you'll find: Specialty chocolates.

The Village Bookstore

201 NW Fourth Street, No. 105, Grand Rapids, MN 55744
218-326-9458

What you'll find: Books, puzzles, calendars, and greeting cards.

Yarnworks

2101 Pokegama Avenue S., Grand Rapids, MN 55744

218-326-9339•www.yarnshopknitting.com

What you'll find: Yarn accessories for knitting, crocheting, and spinning.

MOORHEAD

The Classic

420 Center Avenue, Moorhead, MN 56560

218-236-1110

What you'll find: Women's clothes, accessories, and gifts.

Hi Way 75 Collectibles

713 US Highway 75 N., Moorhead, MN 56560

218-287-0075

What you'll find: Antiques.

Moorhead Antique Mall

2811 SE Main Avenue, Moorhead, MN 56560

218-287-1313•www.moorheadantiquemall.com

What you'll find: Furniture, antiques, and collectibles.

My Best Friend's Closet

11 Ninth Street S., Moorhead, MN 56560

218-236-6937•www.mybestfriendscloset.biz

What you'll find: Women's consignment clothes, jewelry, purses, accessories, and gifts.

DETROIT LAKES

Back Porch Quilts
24047 US Highway 10 W., Detroit Lakes, MN 56501
218-844-6540•www.backporchquilts.com

What you'll find: Fabrics, patterns, and notions.

Detroit Lakes Floral
833 Washington Avenue, Detroit Lakes, MN 56501
218-847-9491•www.detroitlakesfloral.com

What you'll find: Flowers, gifts, home décor, collectibles, and balloons.

Gifts of Flavor
915 Washington Avenue, Detroit Lakes, MN 56501
218-334-2246•www.giftsofflavor.com

What you'll find: Gift baskets.

Ginny's Boutique
813 Washington Avenue, Detroit Lakes, MN 56501
218-846-1817

What you'll find: Women's clothes, shoes, jewelry, accessories, handbags, and gifts.

Price's Fine Jewelry
805 Washington Avenue, Detroit Lakes, MN 56501
218-847-5309 • www.prices-finejewelry.com

What you'll find: Fine diamonds.

The Red Willow
1160 Washington Avenue, Detroit Lakes, MN 56501
218-847-6297

What you'll find: Home décor, kitchen items, jewelry, purses, and gifts.

PARK RAPIDS

Avant Garde on Main
105 S. Main Avenue, Park Rapids MN 56470
218-237-5990 • www.avantgardeonmain.com

What you'll find: Women's and children's clothing and accessories.

Beagle Books
112 Third Street W., Park Rapids, MN 56470
218-237-2665 • www.beagle-books.com

What you'll find: Fiction, nonfiction, nature, regional authors, and children's books; toys; music; maps; art; and gifts.

Irene's Favorite Things

610½ First Street E., Park Rapids, MN 56470
218-732-1121 • www.irenesfavoritethings.com

What you'll find: Finnish and Scandinavian gifts and glassware.

Riverbend Home Expressions

207 S. Main Avenue, Park Rapids MN 56470
218-237-7777 • www.riverbendparkrapids.com

What you'll find: Home furnishings, accessories, gourmet foods, gifts, housewares, children's toys, children's clothing, and wine and bar accessories.

Sister Wolf Books

20471 Minnesota Highway 226, Park Rapids, MN 56470
218-732-7565 • www.sisterwolfbooks.com

What you'll find: Books, coffee bar, gifts, games, and journals.

Summerhill Farm

24013 US Highway 71, Park Rapids, MN 56470
218-732-3865 • www.summerhill-farm.com

What you'll find: Eight specialty shops for clothing, home accessories, specialty foods, gifts, and toys.

Utke's Country Pine Furnishings
21697 US Highway 71, Park Rapids, MN 56470
218-732-3860

What you'll find: Pine furniture, log furniture, North Woods gifts and accessories, outdoor cedar furniture, kayaks, and swim rafts.

AKELEY

Blue Sky Beads
29029 County Road 33, Akeley, MN 56433
218-652-3212 • www.blueskybeads.net

What you'll find: Fairy houses, photography, garden art, handmade beads, pendants, tear bottles, and beading supplies.

WALKER

Book World
410 Minnesota Avenue, Walker, MN 56484
218-547-2743 • www.bookworldstores.com

What you'll find: Books, magazines, cards, and stuffed animals.

Christmas Point Wild Rice Co. & Gifts
523 Minnesota Avenue, Walker, MN 56484
218-547-2170 • www.christmaspoint.com

What you'll find: Jewelry, purses, gifts, furniture, coffee shop, and clothing.

Heritage Arts & Gifts
103 S. Fifth Street, Walker, MN 56484
218-547-3501

What you'll find: Gifts, jewelry, home accessories, antiques, and silk floral.

LA~CE
104 N. Fifth Street, Walker, MN 56484
218-547-2420•www.lacegiftsandclothing.com

What you'll find: Gifts, home décor, and women's apparel.

Main Stream
513 Minnesota Avenue W., Walker, MN 56484
218-547-3166

What you'll find: Women's clothes, shoes, purses, and accessories.

Northern Exposure
506 Minnesota Avenue, Walker, MN 56484
218-547-3440

What you'll find: Northern furniture, moccasins, boots, wine accessories, a Christmas room, a garden room, and rugs.

MOOSE LAKE

Beaver Tracks LTD
4535 S. Arrowhead Lane, Moose Lake, MN 55767
218-485-4624 • www.beavertracks.net

What you'll find: Custom-made shoes, boots, and moccasins.

Kathy's Country Square
100 Hillside Terrace, Moose Lake, MN 55767
218-485-8231

What you'll find: Quilts, antiques, and home décor.

L & D Embroidery
4174 County Road 8, Moose Lake, MN 55767
218-485-4050

What you'll find: Custom embroidery.

Peggy's Consignment Boutique
441 Arrowhead Lane, Moose Lake, MN 55767
218-485-4655

What you'll find: Bridal wear and antiques.

Sonshine Closet
620 Folz Boulevard, Moose Lake, MN 55767
218-485-5758

What you'll find: Clothes, shoes, accessories, gifts, electronics, and toys.

SANDSTONE

All That Floral & Gifts
107 Third Street, Sandstone, MN 55072
320-245-3181

What you'll find: Flowers and gifts.

Cheri's Flower Baskets
322 Commercial Avenue, Sandstone, MN 55072
320-245-2443 • www.cherisflowerbasket.com

What you'll find: Gifts, cards, home décor, flowers, plants, jewelry, and homemade fudge.

Country Bargains
418 Main Street, Sandstone, MN 55072
320-216-7160

What you'll find: New and used clothes, books, furniture, household items, pictures, and home décor.

HINCKLEY

Antiques America
113 Weber Avenue S., Hinckley, MN 55037
320-384-7272

What you'll find: Antiques and collectibles.

The Grindstone Greenhouse & Giftshop
21594 River Chase Road, Hinckley, MN 55037
320-384-7661

What you'll find: Flowers, plants, and home and garden décor.

Quickstitch Sew & Whatknots
102 Old Highway 61 N., Hinckley, MN 55037
320-282-8431

What you'll find: Sewing shop, notions, alterations, and collectibles.

Tobies Boutique and Gift Shop
404 Fire Monument Road, Hinckley, MN 55037
320-384-6174 • www.tobies.com/F_Giftshop.htm

What you'll find: Clothes, jewelry, accessories, home décor, fragrance, music, and books.

Velvet Moose
127 Main Street E., Hinckley, MN 55037
320-384-0267 • www.hinckleymnfloral.com

What you'll find: Flowers and gifts.

PINE CITY

The Creeks Edge
6861 Minnesota Highway 70, Pine City, MN 55063
320-629-3680

What you'll find: Home and North Woods decor, bedding, bath linens, jewelry, purses, scarves, and gifts.

Pine Center for the Arts
265 Fifth Street SE, Pine City, MN 55063
320-629-4924•www.pinecenter.org

What you'll find: Art gallery with featured artist.

Serendipity Home Decor & Gifts
540 Main Street S., Pine City, MN 55063
320-629-2888

What you'll find: Home décor, jewelry, books, works by local artists, and gifts.

BRECKENRIDGE

Breckenridge Drug
116 Fifth Street N., Breckenridge, MN 56520
218-643-5411

What you'll find: Gifts and pharmacy.

Buds Blooms & Boutique
73 Minnesota Avenue, Breckenridge, MN 56520
218-643-2837

What you'll find: Fresh flowers, plants, and gifts.

State and National Parks and Forests

Lake Bronson State Park

3793 230th Street (County Road 28), Lake Bronson, MN 56734
218-754-2200 • www.dnr.state.mn.us/state_parks/lake_bronson

Amenities: Swimming, fishing, boating, camping, picnicking, hiking, biking, cross-country skiing, and snowmobiling.
Features you'll appreciate: One of the campground areas allows camping on the prairie.
Directions: Two miles east of the town of Lake Bronson with park access on County Highway 28.

Hayes Lake State Park

48990 County Road 4, Roseau, MN 56751
218-425-7504
www.dnr.state.mn.us/state_parks/hayes_lake/index.html

Amenities: Swimming, canoeing, camping, and trails for hiking, skiing, snowmobiling, and horseback riding.
Features you'll appreciate: Motor use on Hayes Lake is restricted to electric motors only.
Directions: Fifteen miles south of Roseau on Minnesota Highway 89, then nine miles east on County Road 4.

Zippel Bay State Park

684 Fifty-Fourth Avenue NW, Williams, MN 56686
218-783-6252
www.dnr.state.mn.us/state_parks/zippel_bay/index.html

Amenities: Camping, fishing, beaches, birdwatching, and winter activities.
Features you'll appreciate: Zippel Bay State Park is located on one of the world's largest lakes, Lake of the Woods.

Directions: From the west end of Baudette, take Minnesota Highway 172 ten miles north to County Road 8. Go west for six miles to park entrance.

Franz Jevne State Park
10218 E. Minnesota Highway 11, Birchdale, MN 56629
218-783-6252
www.dnr.state.mn.us/state_parks/franz_jevne/index.html

Amenities: Fishing, hiking, picnicking, and camping.
Features you'll appreciate: Views of Ontario and the Rainy River.
Directions: East of Birchdale on Highway 11.

Old Mill State Park
33489 240th Avenue NW, Argyle, MN 56713
218-437-8174
www.dnr.state.mn.us/state_parks/old_mill/index.html

Amenities: Swimming beach, picnicking, campgrounds, hiking, cross-country ski trails, sliding hill, and a warming house.
Features you'll appreciate: Enjoy the old flour mill and log cabin.
Directions: From Argyle, go twelve miles east on County Road 4, then one mile north on County Road 4 to County Road 39.

Voyageurs National Park
3131 US Highway 53 S., International Falls, MN 56649
218-283-6600 or 218-286-5258•www.nps.gov/voya

Amenities: Hiking, cross-country skiing, snowshoeing, snowmobiling, ice fishing, houseboating, fishing, kayaking, canoeing, and rowboating.

Features you'll appreciate: Nine hiking trails within Voyageurs National Park are accessible by water and land. Pets are not permitted on park hiking trails.

Directions: Five hours north of Minneapolis-St. Paul via Interstate 35 and Highway 53. The Rainy Lake Visitor Center is about twelve miles east of International Falls off Minnesota Highway 11, turn right on County Road 96 (Park Road). Kabetogama Lake Visitor Center is about twenty-five miles south of International Falls; turn off Highway 53 onto County Highway 122.

Boundary Waters Canoe Area Wilderness
Headquarters, 8901 Grand Avenue Place, Duluth, MN 55808
218-626-4300
www.dnr.state.mn.us/canoeing/bwca/index.html

Amenities: More than one million acres, the wilderness extends 150 miles along the international boundary adjacent to Canada's Quetico Provincial Park and is bordered on the west by Voyageurs National Park. There are 1,200 miles of canoe routes, twelve hiking trails, and more than 2,000 designated campsites.

Features you'll appreciate: Permits are required year-round for day and overnight visitors.

Directions: Located in the northern third of the Superior National Forest in northeastern Minnesota. Popular entry points include lakes near Ely, Sawbill Lake near Tofte, and Saganaga and Seagull lakes at the end of the Gunflint Trail.

Superior National Forest
Headquarters, 8901 Grand Avenue Place, Duluth, MN 55808
218-626-4300•www.cwcs.org/superior.html

Amenities: Hiking, hunting, fishing, biking, horseback riding, cross-country skiing, snowmobile, ATV riding, 2,000 miles of trails, camping (twenty-three fee campgrounds, eighteen rustic campgrounds, and more than 277 backcountry campsites), boating, fishing, swimming, or picnicking at one of seventy-seven lake accesses, thirteen fishing piers, ten swimming beaches, twenty-two picnic areas.

Features you'll appreciate: Hunting is allowed on all Superior National Forest lands, including the Boundary Waters Canoe Area Wilderness, except within the limits of developed recreation sites such as campgrounds and boating sites.

Directions: 150 miles along the United States-Canadian border in northeastern Minnesota.

Soudan Underground Mine State Park
1379 Stuntz Bay Road, Soudan, MN 55782
218-753-2245
www.dnr.state.mn.us/state_parks/
soudan_underground_mine/index.html

Amenities: Hiking trails, wildlife observations, historic site, and birdwatching.

Features you'll appreciate: Soudan Underground Mine tour.

Directions: From US Highway 169 in Soudan, follow the directional signs.

Bear Head Lake State Park
9301 Bear Head State Park Road, Ely, MN 55731
218-365-7229
www.dnr.state.mn.us/state_parks/bear_head_lake/index.html

Amenities: Camping, fishing, hiking trails, and twenty-three miles of lakeshore.

Features you'll appreciate: Rent a three-bedroom guest house or camper cabin any season of the year.

Directions: From Tower, take US Highway 169 east nine miles to County Highway 128, then go south seven miles to the park.

Lake Bemidji State Park
3401 State Park Road NE, Bemidji, MN 56601
218-308-2300
www.dnr.state.mn.us/state_parks/lake_bemidji/index.html

Amenities: Swimming, boating, fishing, birdwatching, hiking, camping, biking, picnicking, snowmobiling, and cross-country skiing.
Features you'll appreciate: Year-round naturalist-led activities.
Directions: Ten minutes north of Bemidji off US Highway 71.

Chippewa National Forest
200 Ash Avenue NW, Cass Lake, MN 56633
218-335-8600 • www.fs.usda.gov/Chippewa

Amenities: Beaches and dunes, bicycling, camping and cabins, climbing, hiking, fishing, horse riding, hunting, nature viewing, outdoor learning, water activities, and winter sports.
Features you'll appreciate: Twenty-one developed campgrounds located on the major lakes, primitive campsites, 298 miles of nonmotorized trails, and 315 miles of motorized trails.
Directions: Obtain detailed maps and information from forest headquarters in Cass Lake near the intersection of US Highway 2 and Minnesota Highway 371.

Schoolcraft State Park
9042 Schoolcraft Lane NE, Deer River, MN 56636
218-247-7215
www.dnr.state.mn.us/state_parks/schoolcraft/index.html

Amenities: Camping, hiking, canoeing, picnicking, and fishing.
Features you'll appreciate: A trail system leads hikers through the virgin pine forest that includes a white pine more than 300 years old.
Directions: From US Highway 2 in Grand Rapids, go west and take Minnesota Highway 6 south to County Road 28 west (it turns into County Road 65 west), then go north on County Road 74.

Hill Annex Mine State Park
880 Gary Street, Calumet, MN 55716
218-247-7215
www.dnr.state.mn.us/state_parks/hill_annex_mine/index.html

Amenities: Clubhouse museum, picnicking, historic site, and scenic overlook.
Features you'll appreciate: Hill Annex Mine State Park offers two different tours: the Fossil Hunt and the Historic Mine Tour.
Directions: From US Highway 169 in Calumet, go north on Gary Street about five blocks to the end of the street.

Scenic State Park
56956 Scenic Highway 7, Bigfork, MN 56628
218-743-3362 • www.dnr.state.mn.us/state_parks/scenic/index.html

Amenities: Camping, hiking, fishing, and canoeing.
Features you'll appreciate: Overnight facilities include campsites (boat-in, drive-in, backpack) and a cabin.
Directions: Seven miles east of Bigfork on County Road 7.

McCarthy Beach State Park
7622 McCarthy Beach Road, Side Lake, MN 55781
218-254-7979
www.dnr.state.mn.us/state_parks/mccarthy_beach/index.html

Amenities: Swimming beach, hiking, picnicking, hiking, horse trails, cross-country skiing, and snowmobiling.

Features you'll appreciate: Sturgeon Lake's sandy beach was rated one of the top seventeen beaches in North America by *Highways Magazine*.

Directions: From Hibbing, take US Highway 169 north to County Road 5, then follow that north fifteen miles to the park.

Grand Portage State Park
9393 E. Minnesota Highway 61, Grand Portage, MN 55605
218-475-2360
www.dnr.state.mn.us/state_parks/grand_portage/index.html

Amenities: Minnesota's highest waterfall, hiking, and picnicking.

Features you'll appreciate: The park, for day-use only, lies within the Grand Portage Indian Reservation and is bordered by Canada on the north and east. Lake Superior is one mile east of the park.

Directions: From Grand Marais, north on Highway 61 for thirty-six miles to the US-Canadian border. The park entrance is on the west side of the highway, just before you come to the US Customs Station.

Judge C.R. Magney State Park
4051 E. Minnesota Highway 61, Grand Marais, MN 55604
218-387-3039
www.dnr.state.mn.us/state_parks/judge_cr_magney/index.html

Amenities: Waterfalls, trout fishing, camping, hiking, picnicking, hiking trails, and wildlife observation.

Features you'll appreciate: Most popular hike leads from the trailhead upstream along the Brule River to Devil's Kettle.
Directions: Fourteen miles northeast of Grand Marais on Highway 61.

Cascade River State Park
3481 W. Minnesota Highway 61, Lutsen, MN 55612
218-387-3053
www.dnr.state.mn.us/state_parks/cascade_river/index.html

Amenities: Hiking, camping, skiing, fishing, and waterfalls.
Features you'll appreciate: Trails connect with the Superior Hiking Trail and the North Shore State Trail.
Directions: Ten miles southwest of Grand Marais on Highway 61.

George H. Crosby Manitou State Park
7616 County Road 7, Finland, MN 55603
218-226-6365
www.dnr.state.mn.us/state_parks/george_crosby_manitou/index.html

Amenities: Camping, hiking, waterfalls, and wildlife.
Features you'll appreciate: The trails in the park are carved through a forest of fir, cedar, spruce, and northern hardwoods.
Directions: From Minnesota Highway 61, turn inland at Illgen City on Minnesota Highway 1 to Finland, then go seven miles north on County Road 7.

Temperance River State Park
7620 W. Minnesota Highway 61, Schroeder, MN 55613
218-663-7476
www.dnr.state.mn.us/state_parks/temperance_river/index.html

Amenities: Rock climbing, hiking, fishing, and camping.
Features you'll appreciate: Winter activities include cross-country skiing and snowmobiling.
Directions: Entrance is one mile north of Schroeder on Highway 61.

Tettegouche State Park
5702 Minnesota Highway 61, Silver Bay, MN 55614
218-226-6365
www.dnr.state.mn.us/state_parks/tettegouche/index.html

Amenities: Hiking, camping, rock climbing, and cross-country skiing. Waterfalls, lakes, and Lake Superior shoreline.
Features you'll appreciate: Known for rock climbing and birdwatching in the spring, summer, and fall.
Directions: Entrance to the park is four-and-a-half miles northeast of Silver Bay on Highway 61.

Split Rock Lighthouse State Park
3755 Split Rock Lighthouse Road, Two Harbors, MN 55616
218-226-6377
www.dnr.state.mn.us/state_parks/Split_rock_lighthouse/index.html

Amenities: Tent camping and cart-in sites, cross-country skiing, waterfalls, historic lighthouse and history center tours, and picnicking.

Features you'll appreciate: On the North Shore of Lake Superior and known for its historic lighthouse.

Directions: Twenty miles northeast of Two Harbors on Minnesota Highway 61.

Buffalo River State Park
565 155th Street S., Glyndon, MN 56547
218-498-2124
www.dnr.state.mn.us/state_parks/buffalo_river/index.html

Amenities: Swimming beach, camping, fishing, picnicking, and native prairie landscape.

Features you'll appreciate: A picnic area, swimming area, and campground are located along the Buffalo River.

Directions: From Moorhead, go fourteen miles east on US Highway 10 and follow the signs to the park.

Itasca State Park
36750 Main Park Drive, Park Rapids, MN 56470
218-699-7251
www.dnr.state.mn.us/state_parks/itasca/index.html

Amenities: Minnesota's oldest state park, established in 1891, totals more than 32,000 acres and includes more than 100 lakes. Activities include camping, hiking, biking, fishing, swimming, wilderness drive, boat tours, historic sites, visitor center, and naturalist programs. Famed as headwaters of the Mississippi River. Lodging options include suites, cabins, and hostel. Boat, motor, pontoon, paddleboat, kayak, canoe, and bike rentals. Gifts and groceries available.

Features you'll appreciate: Wireless Internet access at certain locations.

Directions: South entrance to the park is twenty-three miles north of Park Rapids on US Highway 71. From Bemidji, the east entrance is thirty miles south on Highway 71 and one-tenth mile north on Minnesota Highway 200. The north entrance is twenty miles south of Bagley on Minnesota highways 92 and 200.

Jay Cooke State Park
780 E. Minnesota Highway 210, Carlton, MN 55718
218-384-4610
www.dnr.state.mn.us/state_parks/jay_cooke/index.html

Amenities: Picnic area and picnic shelters: Oldenburg Point shelter and the River Inn shelter, volleyball, horseshoes, camping, and hiking.
Features you'll appreciate: Park trails link up to the Willard Munger State Trail at the north edge of the park.
Directions: From Interstate 35, take Exit 235 toward Carlton and go three miles east of Carlton on Highway 210.

Moose Lake State Park
4252 County Road 137, Moose Lake, MN 55767
218-485-5420
www.dnr.state.mn.us/state_parks/moose_lake/index.html

Amenities: Camping, canoeing, fishing and fishing pier, and wildflower and wildlife viewing.
Features you'll appreciate: Two miles west of the park you will find the Willard Munger State Trail.
Directions: From Interstate 35, go a quarter-mile east at Exit 214 and go east on County Road 137 until you see the park signs.

Banning State Park

61101 Banning Park Road, Sandstone, MN 55072
320-245-2668
www.dnr.state.mn.us/state_parks/banning/index.html

Amenities: On the Kettle River, visit ruins of the Sandstone Quarry. Activities include hiking, canoeing and kayaking, cross-country skiing, and Wolf Creek Falls.

Features you'll appreciate: Stay at the new camper cabin (sleeps five people), which includes bunk beds, a table, and benches.

Directions: From Interstate 35, take Exit 195 and follow signs to the park.

St. Croix State Park

30065 St. Croix Park Road, Hinckley, MN 55037
320-384-6591
www.dnr.state.mn.us/state_parks/st_croix/index.html

Amenities: Camping, extensive trail system, canoeing, bird and wildlife observation, and a fire tower.

Features you'll appreciate: St. Croix has more than 34,000 acres and two great rivers: St. Croix River (National Scenic Riverway) and Kettle River (State Wild and Scenic River).

Directions: From Interstate 35, take Exit 183 at Hinckley and go fifteen miles east on Minnesota Highway 48, then five miles south on County Road 22.

Winter Activities

CROSS-COUNTRY SKI TRAILS AND SNOWSHOEING

Hayes Lake State Park
48990 Country Road 4, Roseau, MN 56751
218-425-7504
www.dnr.state.mn.us/state_parks/hayes_lake/trails.html#winter

What you'll find: Eleven miles of trail, classic track and skate ski. Vault toilets in day-use area.

Zippel Bay State Park
3684 Fifty-Fourth Avenue NW, Williams, MN 56686
218-783-6252
www.dnr.state.mn.us/state_parks/zippel_bay/index.html

What you'll find: Nine miles of classic cross-country trails, three miles of trails for skate skiing, restroom facilities. Parking permit required.

Voyageurs National Park
3131 US Highway 53 S., International Falls, MN 56649
218-283-6600
www.nps.gov/voya/planyourvisit/winter-trails.htm

What you'll find: Three groomed cross-country skiing trails equaling more than thirty-seven miles, five miles of snowshoeing across three trails, and Rainy Lake Visitor Center. Free entrance to the park, free snowshoe rental, free children's cross-country equipment rental, and adult cross-country equipment rental.

Old Mill State Park
33489 240th Avenue NW, Argyle, MN 56713
218-437-8174
www.dnr.state.mn.us/state_parks/old_mill/trails.html#winter

What you'll find: Seven miles of trails, visitor center, and restroom facilities. Parking permit required.

Scenic State Park
56956 Scenic Highway 7, Bigfork, MN 56628
218-743-3362
www.dnr.state.mn.us/state_parks/scenic/trails.html

What you'll find: Six miles of cross-country trails, three miles of which are ungroomed. Snowshoeing allowed everywhere in park except cross-country trails. Permit required to enter state park, but day permit available. Ski pass also required.

Banadad Ski Trail
11 Poplar Creek Drive, Grand Marais, MN 55604
218-388-9476•www.banadad.org/trail.html

What you'll find: More than twenty-five miles of trails on the first carbon-neutral Nordic ski trails. Ski pass required for sixteen and older skiers.

Pincushion Mountain Ski Trail
County Roads 53 and 12, Grand Marias, MN 55604
218-387-2969 or 218-387-3373•www.pincushiontrails.org

What you'll find: More than fifteen miles of groomed Nordic skiing trails, one-mile lit trail for night skiing, and warming house.

Cascade River State Park
3481 W. Minnesota Highway 61, Lutsen, MN 55612-9535
218-387-3053
www.dnr.state.mn.us/state_parks/cascade_river/trails.html#winter

What you'll find: Almost six miles of tracked trails and a skating loop. Snowshoeing allowed everywhere, with snowshoe rental available at Tettegouche State Park. Permit required to enter state park, but day permit available. Ski pass also required.

Lutsen Mountains
129 Ski Hill Road, Lutsen, MN 55612
218-663-7281
www.lutsen.com/winter/mountain_info/nordic_skiing.cfm

What you'll find: More than two miles of groomed, tracked cross-country trails for classic or skate skiing, accessible by chairlift with a Nordic ticket. Cross-country ski equipment rental available.

Flathorn/Gegoka Trail
Isabella, MN 55614
218-353-0707 or 877-353-0707
www.nationalforestlodge.com/what_to_do.htm

What you'll find: Almost twenty miles of groomed trails for classic skiing, visitor center, skate skiing, and restroom facilities. Ski pass is required.

Lake Bemidji State Park

300 Bemidji Avenue, Bemidji, MN 56601
218-759-0164
www.dnr.state.mn.us/state_parks/lake_bemidji/trails.html#winter

What you'll find: Eleven miles groomed for classical skiing.

Buena Vista Ski Area

19600 Irvine Avenue NW, Bemidji, MN 56601
218-243-2231 • buenavistaskiarea.blogspot.com/p/x-c-trails.html

What you'll find: More than fifteen miles of trails for track-set and skate skiing, and ski chalet with restroom facilities.

Chippewa National Forest

200 Ash Avenue NW, Cass Lake, MN 56633
218-335-8600
www.dnr.state.mn.us/state_parks/lake_bemidji/index.html

What you'll find: Eleven miles of trails for classical skiing, visitor center, and warming house with restroom facilities.

Carey Lake Ski Trail

401 E. Twenty-First Street, Hibbing MN 55742
218-263-8851 • www.hibbingnordic.org

What you'll find: Eighteen miles of groomed, classic, and skate-skiing trails. Snowshoeing allowed except on cross-country trails. Snowshoeing and cross-country skiing equipment rental is available. Ski pass required.

George H. Crosby Manitou State Park
7616 County Road 7, Finland, MN 55603
218-226-6365
www.dnr.state.mn.us/state_parks/george_crosby_
manitou/trails.html#winter

What you'll find: Ungroomed trails for cross-country skiing. Snowshoeing allowed everywhere with snowshoe rental available at Tettegouche State Park. Permit required to enter state park, but day permit available. Ski pass also required.

Tettegouche State Park
5702 Minnesota Highway 61, Silver Bay, MN 55614
218-226-6365
www.dnr.state.mn.us/state_parks/tettegouche/trails.html#winter

What you'll find: More than fifteen miles of classic trails with almost five miles of skate-skiing trail and visitor center with restrooms. Snowshoeing allowed everywhere in park except cross-country trails. Permit required to enter state park, but day permit available. Ski pass also required.

Temperance River State Park
7620 W. Minnesota Highway 61, Schroeder, MN 55613
218-663-7476
www.dnr.state.mn.us/state_parks/
temperance_river/trails.html#winter

What you'll find: Seventeen miles of ungroomed cross-country ski trails. Snowshoeing allowed in park. Permit required to enter state park, but day permit available. Ski pass also required.

Gooseberry Falls State Park
3206 E. Minnesota Highway 61, Two Harbors, MN 55616
218-834-3855
www.dnr.state.mn.us/state_parks/
gooseberry_falls/trails.html#winter

What you'll find: More than twelve miles of groomed cross-country trail for classic skiing, visitor center, and warming house. Permit required to enter state park, but day permit available. Ski pass also required.

Split Rock Lighthouse State Park
3755 Split Rock Lighthouse Road, Two Harbors, MN 55616
218-226-3065
www.dnr.state.mn.us/state_parks/
Split_rock_lighthouse/trails.html#winter

What you'll find: Eight miles of classic, groomed ski trails and trail center with restrooms. Snowshoeing allowed everywhere in park except cross-country trails. Permit required to enter state park, but day permit available. Ski pass also required.

Snowflake Nordic Center
4348 Rice Lake Road, Duluth, MN 55811
218-726-1550 or 218-728-5068
www.skiduluth.com/?page_id=4

What you'll find: More than nine miles of groomed skiing trails, biathalon range, warming chalet, and waxing room. Equipment rental and lessons are available. Ski pass required.

Dunton Lock County Park
200 State Street E., Detroit Lakes, MN 56501
218-846-2612 or 218-847-0099
www.co.becker.mn.us/dept/parks_recreation/dunton_locks.aspx

What you'll find: Almost four miles of cross-country trails. Ski pass not required.

Itasca State Park
36750 Main Park Drive, Park Rapids, MN 56470
218-266-2100 • www.dnr.state.mn.us/state_parks/itasca/trails.html

What you'll find: Twenty-eight groomed miles of trails for classic and skate skiing. Five snowshoeing trails are available and snowshoeing is allowed throughout the park, except for groomed trails and roads.

Soaring Eagles Trail
US Highway 71, Park Rapids, MN 56470
218-732-9513 • www.itascatur.org/ski.html

What you'll find: More than six groomed miles of trails for classic and skate skiing, warming house, and free equipment rental for youth or adult groups. Ski pass required for sixteen and older skiers.

Deep Portage Conservation Reserve
2197 Nature Center Drive, Hackensack, MN 56452
218-682-2325 • www.deep-portage.org/trails.html

What you'll find: Eleven miles of marked trails for cross-country skiing, Interpretive Center with restroom facilities.

DOWNHILL SKIING AND SNOWBOARDING

Giants Ridge Golf & Ski Resort
6325 Wynne Creek Drive, Biwabik, MN 55708
218-865-3000 or 800-688-7669•www.giantsridge.com

What you'll find: Downhill skiing: thirty-five trails, snowmaking, 500-foot vertical, longest run is 4,500 feet, five chairlifts, one surface lift, night skiing.

Lutsen Mountains
467 Ski Hill Road, Lutsen, MN 55612
218-724-9832•www.lutsen.com

What you'll find: 986-foot vertical drop, ninety-two runs on four mountains, longest run is two miles, seven double chairlifts, one triple chairlift, one ski and snowboard magic carpet, capacity of 10,000 skiers per hour, and sixty acres of tree-skiing runs.

Buena Vista Ski Area
19600 Irvine Avenue NW, Bemidji, MN 56601
218-243-2231 or 800-766-9919•www.bvskiarea.com

What you'll find: Sixteen runs with 230-foot vertical drop, longest run is 2,000 feet, six lifts, 100 percent snowmaking, and two terrain parks for skiers and snowboarders.

Chester Bowl Ski Area
1801 E. Skyline Drive, Duluth, MN 55812
218-724-9832• www.chesterbowl.org

What you'll find: Three main runs, 175-foot vertical drop, longest run is 800 feet, double chairlift, capacity of 960 skiers per hour, and four ski jumps in 119-acre park.

Spirit Mountain Ski and Recreation
9500 Spirit Mountain Place, Duluth, MN 55810
218-628-2891 or 800-642-6377•www.spiritmt.com

What you'll find: 700-foot vertical drop, twenty-two runs, longest run is 5,400 feet, one super pipe, 175 skiable acres of terrain, five chairlifts, one conveyor lift, one handle tow, and one rope tow.

ICE FISHING

Reel Adventures Fishing Service
620 E. Lake Street, Warroad, MN 56763
218-469-0721•www.reeladventureslow.com

What you'll find: Ice fishing sleeper and day houses rentals on Lake of the Woods, gas heated, eight-hole fish houses, four-by-six man sleepers, Bombardier ride out and back, bait included.

Rich's Ice Fishing
Lake of the Woods, Warroad, MN 56763
218-821-6464•www.richsicefishing.com

What you'll find: Sleeper fish house rental on Lake of the Woods, indoor toilet facilities, heater, lights, cooking stove, cooking and eating utensils, bait and bunks.

Springsteel Resort Inc.
38004 Beach Street, Warroad, MN 56763
218-386-1000•www.springsteelresort.net

What you'll find: Fish house rental on Lake of the Woods, includes bait, transportation, and two holes.

Ballard's Resort
3314 Bur Oak Road NW, Baudette, MN 56623
218-634-1849 or 800-776-2675 • www.ballardsresort.com

What you'll find: Fish house rentals on Lake of the Woods, poles, bait, tackle, and fish processing provided.

Gibbins Fishing
2178 Thirty-Eighth Avenue NW, Baudette, MN 56623
218-634-1589 • www.gibbinsicefishing.com

What you'll find: Sleeper fish house rental on Lake of the Woods, includes bait, transportation, propane heat and lights, stove, oven, utensils, and bunks.

Ken-Mar-Ke Resort
3174 Ken-Mar-Ke Drive NW, Baudette, MN 56623
218-634-2072 or 800-535-8155 • www.ken-mar-keresort.com

What you'll find: Ice fishing cabin rentals on Lake of the Woods, transportation, bait, and equipment provided.

Lyon Sleepers
3029 Twenty-Ninth Avenue NW, Baudette, MN 56623
218-634-1863 or 800-664-3735 • www.lyonsleepers.com

What you'll find: Sleeper fish house rentals on Lake of the Woods, transportation, propane heater and lights, stove, oven, utensils, bunks, toilet, and bait provided. Vexilar fish finder and generator can be rented separately.

Sweet Sleepers
2867 Royal Oak Drive NW, Baudette, MN 56623
218-634-1582 or 888-226-8638, ext. 3091 • www.sweetsleepers.com

What you'll find: Ice fishing house rental with furnaces, cook stoves, restroom, up to six sleeping bunks, televisions, track and four-wheel-drive vehicles, cooking utensils, card table and chairs, and fish cleaning available.

Walleye Retreat, LLC
4074 County Road 8 NW, Baudette, MN 56623
218-634-3126 or 800-726-9042 • www.walleyeretreat.com

What you'll find: Day fish house rentals and sleeper fish house rental on Lake of the Woods. Transportation provided. Sleepers are equipped with stove, propane heat and lights, and utensils.

Wheeler's Point Resort
2604 River Lane, Baudette, MN 56623
218-634-2629 or 800-542-2435 • www.wheelerspoint.com

What you'll find: Sleeper fish house rental on Lake of the Woods, includes bait, transportation, equipped kitchen, indoor restroom, bunks, propane heaters, and lights. Vexilar fish finders are available to rent separately.

Thunderbird Lodge
2170 County Road 139, International Falls, MN 556649
218-286-3151 or 800-351-5133 • www.thunderbirdrainylake.com

What you'll find: Ice fishing house rental on Rainy Lake, food packages, multihole houses, guided fishing, portable fishing houses, and snowmobile rental to reach remote fishing locations.

Bear Paw Guides
26081 Liliput Lane, Waskish, MN 56685
218-647-8562•www.bearpawguides.com

What you'll find: Day fish house and sleeper fish house rentals on Upper Red Lake. Sleepers include bunks, stove, gas heat, lights, fans, and pre-drilled holes.

White Birch Resort
18882 N. Blackduck Lake Drive NE, Blackduck, MN 56630
218-835-4552 or 877-835-4552•www.whitebirchresort.net

What you'll find: Day fish house on Blackduck Lake.

Gus' Place Resort
32228 County Road 39, Deer River, MN 56636
218-246-8520 or 888-246-8520•www.gusplaceresort.com

What you'll find: Portable ice fishing houses rental on Ball Club Lake with plowed lake access and augur rentals.

High Banks Resort
17645 N. High Banks Road NE, Deer River, MN 56636
218-246-2560 or 800-365-2560•www.highbanks.com

What you'll find: Sleeper fish house rental on Lake Winnibigoshish with plowed lake access and winterized fish cleaning house.

Little Winnie Resort
55671 County Road 9, Deer River, MN 56646
218-246-8501 or 800-346-8501 • www.littlewinnie.com

What you'll find: No ice house rental, but an assortment of ice fishing tackle, bait, and equipment.

The Pines Resort
17221 Winnie Dam Road NE, Deer River, MN 56636
218-246-8546 or 800-342-1552 • www.thepinesresort.com

What you'll find: Fish house rental on Lake Winnibigoshish with plowed lake access.

Adventure North Resort
4444 Point Landing Drive NW, Walker, MN 56484
800-294-1532 • www.adventurenorthresort.com

What you'll find: Day fish house on Leech Lake with propane heat, lights, and clean-and-fillet fish packaging included.

The Canoeist.com
701 Seventh Avenue, Two Harbors, MN 55616
218-834-3523 • www.thecanoeist.com

What you'll find: Fish house rental with heater, hand auger, depth finder, rod and tackle, and tip-up rental.

Hi Banks Resort
5392 Fish Lake Dam Road, Duluth, MN 55803
218-721-3355 or 888-924-3355•www.hibanksresort.com

What you'll find: Ice fishing house rental on Fish Lake.

ICE SKATING AND HOCKEY

Roseau Memorial Arena
315 Third Avenue NE, Roseau, MN 56751
218-463-1538•http://city.roseau.mn.us

What you'll find: Ice hockey arena.

Rams Sports Center
809 Sixth Street NE, Roseau, MN 56751
218-463-0022

What you'll find: Ice hockey arena.

The Gardens Arena
707 Elk Street NW, Warroad, MN 56763
218-386-3862

What you'll find: Ice hockey arena.

Baudette Arena
Wilderness Drive and Fifth Street SW, Baudette, MN 56623
218-634-1319

What you'll find: Ice hockey arena.

Holler Hockey Rink

Twentieth Street and Second Avenue, International Falls, MN 56649
218-283-9484
www.ci.international-falls.mn.us/dp-parks.html#sportsfacilities

What you'll find: Outdoor rink.

Kerry Park Arena

Eleventh Street, International Falls, MN 56649
218-283-9484

What you'll find: Ice hockey arena.

Huck Olson Memorial Civic Center

Third Street and Brooks Avenue, Thief River Falls, MN 56701
218-681-1835

What you'll find: Ice hockey arena.

Northop Park Rink

Tenth Street and Labree Avenue N., Thief River Falls, MN 56701
218-681-2519

What you'll find: Outdoor rink.

Ralph Engelstad Arena

Sixth Street and Brooks Avenue, Thief River Falls, MN 56701
218-681-2183 • www.reatrf.com

What you'll find: Ice hockey arena.

Thief River Falls Old Arena
Second Street and Knight Avenue N., Thief River Falls, MN 56701
218-681-2519

What you'll find: Ice hockey arena.

East Grand Forks Civic Center
30 Fifteenth Street NE, East Grand Forks, MN 56721
218-773-1815 • www.egf.mn/index.aspx?NID=305

What you'll find: Ice hockey arena.

VFW Memorial Youth Center
711 Third Street SE, East Grand Forks, MN 56721
218-773-1851 • www.egf.mn/index.aspx?NID=306

What you'll find: Ice hockey arena.

Bemidji Community Arena
3000 Division Street NW, Bemidji, MN 56601
218-444-5661

What you'll find: Ice hockey arena.

Glas Fieldhouse
1500 Birchmont Drive, Bemidji, MN 56601
218-755-3292

What you'll find: Ice hockey arena.

Neilson-Reise Arena
1115 Twenty-Third Street NW, Bemidji, MN 56601
218-751-4541

What you'll find: Ice hockey arena.

Hoyt Lakes Arena
106 Kennedy Memorial Drive, Hoyt Lakes, MN 55750
218-225-2226 • www.hoytlakes.com/recreat/arena/arena.htm

What you'll find: Ice hockey arena.

Chisholm Sports Arena
501 First Street NW, Chisholm, MN 55719
218-254-2635

What you'll find: Ice hockey arena.

Greenhaven Rink
E. Thirty-Seventh Street and Seventh Avenue E., Hibbing, MN 55746
218-263-8851

What you'll find: Outdoor rink.

Hibbing Memorial Ice Arena
400 E. Twenty-Third Street, Hibbing, MN 55746
218-263-4379 • www.hibbing.mn.us

What you'll find: Ice hockey arena.

Kelly Lake Rink
E. Twenty-Eighth Street, Hibbing, MN 55746
218-263-8851

What you'll find: Outdoor rink.

Nashwauk Recreation Complex
200 Fourth Street, Nashwauk, MN 55769
218-885-3763

What you'll find: Ice hockey arena.

Hodgins-Berardo Arena
200 Curley Avenue, Coleraine, MN 55722
218-245-3525

What you'll find: Ice hockey arena.

Lake County Arena
301 Eighth Avenue, Two Harbors, MN 55616
218-834-8339

What you'll find: Ice hockey arena.

Moorhead Sports Center
324 S. Twenty-Fourth Street, Moorhead, MN 56560
218-299-5354 or 218-299-5353
www.ci.moorhead.mn.us/parks/facilities/facilities/facilities.html

What you'll find: Ice hockey arena.

Moorhead Youth Hockey Arena
707 SE Main Avenue, Moorhead, MN 56560
218-233-5021
www.moorheadyouthhockey.com/page/show/39237-home

What you'll find: Ice hockey arena.

Freeman Sports Arena
1300 Rossman Avenue, Detroit Lakes, MN 56501
218-846-7105 • www.ci.detroit-lakes.mn.us/recreation/rec_arena.htm

What you'll find: Ice hockey arena.

Park Rapids Community Center
211 Huntsinger Avenue, Park Rapids, MN 56470
218-732-9179

What you'll find: Ice hockey arena.

AMSOIL Arena
350 Harbor Drive, Duluth, MN 55802
218-722-5573 • www.decc.org

What you'll find: Ice hockey arena.

Fryberger Ice Arena
3211 Allendale Avenue, Duluth, MN 55803
218-724-0094

What you'll find: Ice hockey arena.

Mars Lakeview Arena
1201 Rice Lake Road, Duluth, MN 55811
218-722-4455 • www.marslakeview.com

What you'll find: Ice hockey arena.

Petersen Arena
3501 Grand Avenue, Duluth, MN 55807
218-624-3181

What you'll find: Ice hockey arena.

Hermantown Arena
4309 Ugstad Road, Hermantown, MN 55811
218-729-5493

What you'll find: Ice hockey arena.

Mora Civic Center
701 Union Street S., Mora, MN 55051
320-679-2443

What you'll find: Ice hockey arena.

SLEDDING AND SNOW TUBING

Old Mill State Park
33489 240th Avenue NW, Argyle, MN 56713
218-437-8174 • www.dnr.state.mn.us/state_parks/old_mill/rec.html

What you'll find: Sliding hill.

Giants Ridge Golf & Ski Resort
6325 Wynne Creek Drive, Biwabik, MN 55708
800-688-7669•www.giantsridge.com/winter/tubing

What you'll find: Tube rental and tow rope.

Buena Vista Ski Area
19600 Irvine Avenue NW, Bemidji, MN 56601
218-243-2231 or 800-777-7958

What you'll find: Tube rental.

SNOWMOBILING

Beltrami Island State Forest–East
218-634-2172
www.dnr.state.mn.us/snow_depth/trails.html?facility_id=4103

What you'll find: More than fifty-two miles of groomed trail across mostly flat land. Snowmobile State Trail sticker is required.

Big Bog State Recreation Area
Waskish, MN 56685
218-647-8592
www.dnr.state.mn.us/snow_depth/trails.html?facility_id=4377

What you'll find: Ten miles of groomed trail and part of the grant-in-aid trail system. Snowmobile State Trail sticker is required.

Arrowhead State Trail
650 US Highway 169, Tower, MN 55790
218-753-2580, ext. 250
www.dnr.state.mn.us/snow_depth/trails.html?facility_id=4095

What you'll find: 128 miles of groomed trails. Snowmobile State Trail sticker is required.

Ash River State Forest
650 US Highway 169, Tower, MN 55790
218-753-2580, ext. 2
www.dnr.state.mn.us/snow_depth/trails.html?facility_id=4096

What you'll find: A hilly trail going through forest. The trail is not mechanically groomed.

Bear Head Lake State Park
9301 Bear Head State Road, Ely, MN 55731
218-365-7229
www.dnr.state.mn.us/state_parks/bear_head_lake/trails.html

What you'll find: Groomed trail over hills, and through birch and pine forests. Snowmobile State Trail sticker is required.

George Washington State Forest–Bear Lake Trail
218-999-7923
www.dnr.state.mn.us/snow_depth/trails.html?facility_id=4099

What you'll find: Eleven miles of groomed trail through steep and rocky terrain with multiple lakes and rivers, and a shelter along the trail. Snowmobile State Trail sticker is required.

George Washington State Forest–Circle L
218-999-7923
www.dnr.state.mn.us/snow_depth/trails.html?facility_id=4113

What you'll find: Fifteen miles of groomed trail. Snowmobile State Trail sticker is required.

George Washington State Forest–Thistledew
218-999-7923
www.dnr.state.mn.us/snow_depth/trails.html?facility_id=4194

What you'll find: Ungroomed trail through mature forest, some recently reforested areas, and a shelter along the trail. Snowmobile State Trail sticker is required.

George Washington State Forest–Tim Corey
218-999-7923
www.dnr.state.mn.us/snow_depth/trails.html?facility_id=4195

What you'll find: Seventeen miles of groomed trail that connects with other rails. Shelter along the trail. Snowmobile State Trail sticker is required.

Taconite State Trail–Grand Rapids
1201 US Highway 2, Grand Rapids, MN 55744
218-999-7920
www.dnr.state.mn.us/snow_depth/trails.html?facility_id=4190

What you'll find: 150 miles of groomed trail with shelters along the trail. Snowmobile State Trail sticker is required.

Bemidji-Itasca State Trail
3296 State Park Road NE, Bemidji, MN 56601
218-308-2372
www.dnr.state.mn.us/snow_depth/trails.html?facility_id=4102

What you'll find: Thirty miles of groomed trail across rolling hills. Snowmobile State Trail sticker is required.

Itasca State Park
36750 Main Park Drive, Park Rapids, MN 56470
218-266-2100
www.dnr.state.mn.us/snow_depth/trails.html?facility_id=4136

What you'll find: Thirty-two miles of groomed trail through mixed forests. Snowmobile State Trail sticker is required.

Paul Bunyan State Trail–Walker
Crow Wing State Park (south of Brainerd/Baxter) to Lake Bemidji State Park (north of Bemidji)
218-308-2372
www.dnr.state.mn.us/snow_depth/trails.html?facility_id=4170

What you'll find: Thirty miles of groomed trail with views of lakes and rivers through forests. Snowmobile State Trail sticker is required.

Cascade River State Park
3481 W. Minnesota Highway 61, Lutsen, MN 55612
218-387-3053
www.dnr.state.mn.us/snow_depth/trails.html?facility_id=4112

What you'll find: Two miles of groomed trail through cliff and forest terrain. Snowmobile State Trail sticker is required.

George H. Crosby Manitou State Park
7616 County Road 7, Finland, MN 55603
218-226-6365
www.dnr.state.mn.us/snow_depth/trails.html?facility_id=4115

What you'll find: Groomed trail. Snowmobile State Trail sticker is required.

Gooseberry Falls State Park
3206 E. Minnesota Highway 61, Two Harbors, MN 55616
218-834-3855
www.dnr.state.mn.us/snow_depth/trails.html?facility_id=4128

What you'll find: Three miles of groomed trail follows the Lake Superior shoreline. Snowmobile State Trail sticker is required.

Jay Cooke State Park
780 E. Minnesota Highway 210, Carlton, MN 55718
218-384-4610
www.dnr.state.mn.us/snow_depth/trails.html?facility_id=4137

What you'll find: Twelve miles of partially groomed trail through hills with views of the St. Louis River gorge. Snowmobile State Trail sticker is required.

Banning State Park
61101 Banning Park Road, Sandstone, MN 55072
320-245-2668
www.dnr.state.mn.us/snow_depth/trails.html?facility_id=4097

What you'll find: Five miles of groomed trail and four feet of trail base. Snowmobile State Trail sticker is required.

St. Croix State Park
30065 St. Croix Park Road, Hinckley, MN 55037
320-384-6591
www.dnr.state.mn.us/snow_depth/trails.html?facility_id=4189

What you'll find: Eighty miles of groomed trail. Snowmobile State Trail sticker is required.

WINTER CABINS AND CAMPING

Lake Bronson State Park
3793 230th Street (County Road 28), Lake Bronson, MN 56734
218-754-2200
www.dnr.state.mn.us/state_parks/lake_bronson/seasonal.html

What you'll find: Some of the 157 campsites are available for winter camping, but call ahead. Flush toilets in the visitor center and vault toilets in the park. No showers. Pets welcome, if leashed.

Hayes Lake State Park
48990 County Road 4, Roseau, MN 56751
218-425-7504
www.dnr.state.mn.us/state_parks/hayes_lake/seasonal.html

What you'll find: Contact the park ahead of time to make sure winter camping is available. Water available at the contract station and vault toilets throughout the park. No showers. Pets welcome, if leashed.

Zippel Bay State Park
3684 Fifty-Fourth Avenue NW, Williams, MN 56686
218-783-6252
www.dnr.state.mn.us/state_parks/zippel_bay/seasonal.html

What you'll find: Campground is open year-round. Water available at hand pumps and vault toilets throughout the park. No showers. Pets welcome, if leashed.

Franz Jevne State Park
10218 E. Minnesota Highway 11, Birchdale, MN 56629
218-783-6252
www.dnr.state.mn.us/state_parks/franz_jevne/seasonal.html

What you'll find: Eighteen campsites available year-round. Water available at hand pumps and vault toilets throughout the park. No showers. Pets welcome, if leashed.

Big Bog State Recreation Area
Waskish, MN 56685
218-647-8592
www.dnr.state.mn.us/state_parks/big_bog/camping.html

What you'll find: Five year-round camper cabins with both electricity and heat. Four of the five cabins sleep six people, one cabin sleeps five and is handicap accessible. All cabins have a wood stove. No pets allowed. Vault toilets available. No showers.

Bear Head Lake State Park
9301 Bear Head State Park Road, Ely, MN 55731
218-365-7229
www.dnr.state.mn.us/state_parks/bear_head_lake/seasonal.html

What you'll find: Five year-round camper cabins with both electricity and heat. Three of the five cabins sleep six people; the other two sleep five people and are accessible. Vault toilets available. No showers. No pets allowed.

Lake Bemidji State Park
3401 State Park Road NE, Bemidji, MN 56601
218-308-2300
www.dnr.state.mn.us/state_parks/lake_bemidji/seasonal.html

What you'll find: One nonelectric, drive-in campsite available year-round. Group campsite is available but only access is by foot, ski, or snowshoe. Water available at visitor center and vault toilets throughout the park. No showers. Pets welcome, if leashed.

Scenic State Park
56956 Scenic Highway 7, Bigfork, MN 56628
218-743-3362
www.dnr.state.mn.us/state_parks/scenic/seasonal.html

What you'll find: Electric campsites available year-round. Water available at frost-free hydrant, and vault toilets throughout the park. No showers. Pets welcome, if leashed.

McCarthy Beach State Park
7622 McCarthy Beach Road, Side Lake, MN 55781
218-254-7979
www.dnr.state.mn.us/state_parks/mccarthy_beach/seasonal.html

What you'll find: Eighteen electric walk-in only campsites available year-round. Water available at park office. Vault toilets throughout the park. No showers. Pets welcome, if leashed.

Cascade River State Park
3481 W. Minnesota Highway 61, Lutsen, MN 55612
218-387-3053
www.dnr.state.mn.us/state_parks/cascade_river/seasonal.html

What you'll find: Three nonelectric, tent campsites. Vault toilets available. Warming house with wood stove heat. No showers. Pets welcome, if leashed.

Temperance River State Park
7620 W. Minnesota Highway 61, Schroeder, MN 55613
218-663-7476
www.dnr.state.mn.us/state_parks/temperance_river/seasonal.html

What you'll find: Ten electric campsites available year-round. Vault toilets in park. No showers. Pets welcome, if leashed.

Gooseberry Falls State Park
3206 E. Minnesota Highway 61, Two Harbors, MN 55616
218-834-3855
www.dnr.state.mn.us/state_parks/gooseberry_falls/seasonal.html

What you'll find: Sixty-nine nonelectric, walk-in campsites. Flush toilets in the visitor center and vault toilets in the park. Warming house with wood stove heat. No showers. Pets welcome, if leashed.

Split Rock Lighthouse State Park
3755 Split Rock Lighthouse Road, Two Harbors, MN 55616
218-226-6377
www.dnr.state.mn.us/state_parks/split_rock_lighthouse/seasonal.html

What you'll find: Nonelectric campsites available year-round. Water and flush toilets available at trail center. Vault toilets throughout the park. No showers. Pets welcome, if leashed.

Savanna Portage State Park
55626 Lake Place, McGregor, MN 55760
218-426-3271
www.dnr.state.mn.us/state_parks/savanna_portage/seasonal.html

What you'll find: One year-round camper cabin with heat but no electricity. Cabin sleeps five people and is accessible. Vault toilets available. No showers. No pets allowed. Six backpack sites available year-round.

Jay Cooke State Park
780 E. Minnesota Highway 210, Carlton, MN 55718
218-384-4610
www.dnr.state.mn.us/state_parks/jay_cooke/seasonal.html

What you'll find: Twelve tent sites are available for winter camping, of which six are electrical sites. Flush and vault toilets, and two shelters with fireplaces and electricity available. Vehicle permit required. Pets welcome, if leashed. Also five year-round camper cabins with both electricity and heat. Three of the five cabins sleep six people; the other two cabins sleep five people. No showers. No pets allowed.

Moose Lake State Park
4252 County Road 137, Moose Lake, MN 55767
218-485-5420
www.dnr.state.mn.us/state_parks/moose_lake/seasonal.html

What you'll find: Three electric and two nonelectric campsites available year-round. Flush toilets and water available at park office. Vault toilets throughout the park. No showers. Pets welcome, if leashed.

Banning State Park
61101 Banning Park Road, Sandstone, MN 55072
320-245-2668 • www.dnr.state.mn.us/state_parks/banning/seasonal.html

What you'll find: Two electric and three nonelectric campsites available year-round. Water available at park office. Vault toilets throughout the park. No showers. Pets welcome, if leashed.

WINTER FESTIVALS AND EVENTS

Blizzard Bash
Wigwam Resort
502 Four Mile Bay Drive NW, Baudette, MN 56623
218-634-2168 or 800-448-9260
www.wigwamresortlow.com/events.html

What you'll find: One-day event featuring Tip-Up Derby, ice fishing demonstrations, children's and adult games, and Ice Fishing Expo.

Icebox Days in International Falls
International Falls Area Chamber of Commerce
301 Second Avenue, International Falls, MN 56649
218-283-9400 or 800-325-5766
www.internationalfallsmn.us/iceboxdays.shtml

What you'll find: Four-day event: Freeze Yer Gizzard Blizzard 5K and 10K runs, candlelight skiing in Voyageurs National Park, snow sculpting, frozen turkey bowling, and smoosh races.

Ely Winter Festival
Ely, MN 56433
800-777-7281 • www.elywinterfestival.com

What you'll find: Ten-day event with art walk, crafts fair, sled dog rides, spaghetti dinner, music, and dancing.

Winter Tracks Festival
Cook County Visitors Bureau Grand Marais, MN 55604
218-387-2524 or 800-338-6932•http://donorth.mn/wintertracks/

What you'll find: Ten-day event with professionally groomed trails, candlelight skis, snowshoe hikes, bonfires, and sleigh and snowmobile rides.

Laskiainen Finnish Sliding Festival
3816 Highway 100, Aurora, MN 55705
218-638-2551•www.ironrange.org/attractions/calendar/?312

What you'll find: Two-day event with crafts, music, sports, foods, and sliding.

Winter Frolic
Two Harbors Area Chamber of Commerce
1330 Minnesota Highway 61, Two Harbors, MN 55616
218-834-6200 or 800-777-7384•www.twoharborswinterfrolic.com

What you'll find: Two-day event with parade, smoosh races, outhouse races, photo scavenger hunt, bonfire, music, sliding hill, boot hockey, alumni hockey tournament, vintage snowmobile show, chili cook-off, silent auction, and basket raffles.

American Legion Community Ice Fishing Derby
Park Rapids, MN 56470
800-247-0054•www.parkrapidsfishingderby.com

What you'll find: One-day fishing event with cash and raffle prizes.

Audrey's Purple Dream Fishing Tournament
11th Crow Wing Lake, Akeley, MN 56433
218-652-2465•www.audreyspurpledream.com

What you'll find: One-day fishing event with pancake breakfast, cash and raffle prizes, purple plunge, live music, and dancing.

Eelpout Festival
Walker, MN 56484
www.eelpoutfestival.com/events.html

What you'll find: Three-day event with eelpout angling competition, ice drilling, on-ice auto race, polar plunge, and sled dog races.

The John Beargrease Sled Dog Race
218-722-7631•www.beargrease.com

What you'll find: The John Beargrease Sled Dog Race is a 390-mile race along the North Shore of Lake Superior, which mushers and spectators attend.

Polar Bear Plunge
Lakeside at Canal Park, Canal Park Drive, Duluth, MN 55802
800-783-7732
www.plungemn.org/index.php?page=location&where=duluth

What you'll find: Minnesota law enforcement personnel, individuals, organizations, and businesses support Special Olympics athletes by jumping into frigid Minnesota waters.

Warmer by the Lake Celebration
Bayfront Festival Park, Duluth, MN 55802
800-438-5884 • http://visitduluth.com/featured/warmer-by-the-lake.php

What you'll find: One-day event with ice skating, snowshoeing, marshmallow roasting, and live music. Free hot chocolate and cookies in the warming tent.

Carlton Winterfest
Carlton Area Chamber of Commerce
213 Chestnut Avenue, Carlton, MN 55718
218-384-3322
www.cityofcarlton.com/chambersite/winterfest.htm

What you'll find: Three-day event with chili cook-off, fishing tournament, sled-dog races, and children's activities.

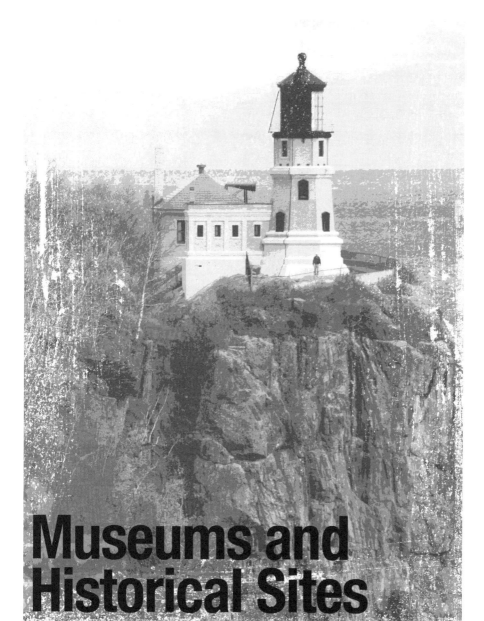

Museums and
Historical Sites

Lake of the Woods County Museum
119 Eighth Avenue SE, Baudette, MN 56623
218-634-1200 • www.lakeofthewoodshistoricalsociety.com

What you'll find: The history of Minnesota's youngest county, including murals, photographs, and artifacts on geology, natural history, early peoples, fur trade, settlement, fishing, logging, farming, and events such as the forest fire of 1910. Displays of early farm equipment, a general store, homestead, and blacksmith shop. Open mid-May through September.

Directions: Just south of Minnesota Highway 11 (Main Street) on Eighth Avenue SE.

Koochiching County Historical Museum
214 Sixth Avenue, in Smokey Bear Park, International Falls, MN 56649
218-283-4316 • www.rainylake.org/thingstodo.html

What you'll find: The Koochiching County Historical Museum contains artifacts and historical materials with exhibits on fur trade, logging, European settlement, and Native American history and culture of the area. Open year-round.

Directions: Take US Highway 53 (Third Avenue) into downtown International Falls and go left on Third Street three blocks to Sixth Avenue.

Bronko Nagurski Museum
214 Sixth Avenue, in Smokey Bear Park, International Falls, MN 56649
218-283-4316
http://bronkonagurski.com/The%20Bronko%20Museum.html

What you'll find: The Bronko Nagurski Museum, the first dedicated to an individual football player, opened as a wing of the Koochiching

County Historical Society in 1993. Exhibits and photographs honor the accomplishments of International Falls' favorite son, who became a University of Minnesota and NFL legend. Open year-round.
Directions: Take US Highway 53 (Third Avenue) into downtown International Falls and go left on Third Street three blocks to Sixth Avenue.

Peder Engelstad Pioneer Village
825 Oakland Park Road, Thief River Falls, MN 56701
218-681-5767
www.visittrf.org/bm/Eat_Sleep_Do/Attractions/Museums/peder-engelstad-pioneer-village.shtml

What you'll find: Named after a local Norwegian immigrant, this turn-of-the-century village includes vintage flower gardens, a museum, and nineteen buildings, including log houses, a blacksmith shop, a general store, barber and beauty shops, two railroad depots, a one-room schoolhouse, a church, and a Victorian home, as well as a building full of farm machinery and antique cars. Open Memorial Day through Labor Day.
Directions: From US Highway 59 in downtown Thief River Falls, go south on Main Avenue/Minnesota Highway 32 about a half-mile and turn left at Oakland Park.

Grand Portage National Monument
170 Mile Creek Road, Grand Portage, MN 55605
218-475-0123 • www.nps.gov/grpo

What you'll find: Guided programs and demonstrations preserve fur trading and Ojibwe heritage. Programs include Three Sisters Native American garden, historic heirloom gardens, furnished structures, area history, historical demonstrations with costumed guides, cooking and baking demonstrations, and birch bark canoe building program. Heritage Visitor Center is open year-round.

Directions: About a half-mile to a mile south of Minnesota Highway 61 at Grand Portage.

Soudan Underground Mine State Park
1379 Stuntz Bay Road, Soudan, MN 55782
218-753-2245
www.dnr.state.mn.us/state_parks/soudan_
underground_mine/index.html

What you'll find: A ninety-minute tour takes visitors a half-mile underground into Minnesota's oldest iron-ore mine, including a stop at a University of Minnesota physics lab. Visitors wear hard hats to ride down 2,341 feet in a cage to level twenty-seven, then ride a rail car back into the mine. Above ground, visitors can tour the dry house, drill shop, crusher house, and engine house, or hike a boardwalk or wooded trails. Tours Memorial Weekend through Labor Day, and limited in September and October.

Directions: From US Highway 169 in Soudan, follow the directional signs.

Ely-Winton History Museum
1900 E. Camp Street, Ely, MN 55731
218-365-3226 • www.vcc.edu/ewhs/

What you'll find: A collection of early Ely photographs and artifacts that tells the story of Native Americans, Scandinavian-Americans, voyageurs, lumbermen, prospectors, and miners who settled in what was a wilderness area.

Directions: On the campus of Vermilion Community College, from US Highway 169 (Sheridan Street), turn left on Seventeenth Avenue and right on E. Camp Street. Open year-round.

Heritage Homestead Tours
7503 Levander Road, Embarrass, MN 55732
218-984-2084
www.embarrass.org/index.php?option=
com_content&task=blogsection&id=5&Itemid=30

What you'll find: Fifteen-mile, three-hour guided tours of restored Finnish homesteads, handcrafted log buildings, and an authentic sauna. Includes the Nelimark Homestead Museum. Memorial Weekend through Labor Day Weekend.
Directions: Start at the visitor's center in Embarrass at the intersection of County Road 21 and Minnesota Highway 135.

Minnesota Discovery Center
1005 Discovery Drive, Chisholm, MN 55719
218-254-7959 or 800-372-6437 • www.mndiscoverycenter.com

What you'll find: The center consists of a park and a research center, as well as a 33,000-square-foot museum that houses exhibits on Iron Range immigrants from Europe and their descendants. Stories document the development of the Iron Range, which would become the nation's largest producer of iron ore, and the life and work of Minnesota's longest-serving governor, Rudy Perpich, an Iron Range native. Open Tuesday–Sunday year-round with additional summer hours.
Directions: From Interstate 35, take Exit 237 to Minnesota Highway 33 at Cloquet and follow that to US Highway 53 and on to Virginia, then take US Highway 169 west to Chisholm. Follow signs to entrance.

Minnesota Museum of Mining

701 W. Lake Street, Chisholm, MN 55719

218-254-5543 or 218-254-2179 • www.mnmuseumofmining.org

What you'll find: This fifteen-acre museum, in a city park surrounded by a rock wall, preserves the history of the iron mining industry in Minnesota and the people who worked in the mines. Visitors begin at a 1933 stone castle, which contains displays of mining history. Once outdoors, visitors can climb on huge mining shovels, and see a 1907 steam locomotive and other heavy equipment. Includes replica of an underground mine and a mining town, a model train exhibit, and even the first Greyhound bus.

Directions: From US Highway 169 across from the Minnesota Discovery Center, turn onto Ironworld Road and follow one-tenth mile to stop sign. Go right on Minnesota Highway 73 N. and follow it six-tenths of a mile to the museum sign and turn left.

Wirtanen Pioneer Farm

5321 Markham Road, Makinen, MN 55763

218-638-2859 • http://wirtanenfarm.org

What you'll find: Restored forty-acre pioneer farmstead now an open-air museum whose buildings are of Finnish hand-hewn log construction. The site's mission is to promote Finnish immigrant culture and history.

Directions: About eighteen miles south of Biwabik on the Vermilion Trail and right on County Road 339 (Markham Road).

Finland Minnesota Historical Society
5653 County Road 6, Finland, MN 55603
218-353-7380•www.finlandmnhistoricalsociety.com

What you'll find: The Finland Minnesota Heritage Site includes a new museum, the John Pine forty-acre homestead, and a memorial orchard. The site celebrates the settlement history of eastern Lake County and its pioneer families. Open Wednesday–Sunday, mid-May to October.
Directions: From Minnesota Highway 61, turn left on Little Marais Road (County Road 6) and ago about three miles.

Itasca County Historical Society
10 NW Fifth Street, Grand Rapids, MN 55744
218-326-6431•http://itascahistorical.org

What you'll find: Located in the restored 1895 Old Central School, exhibits interpret life at the turn of the century: Native Americans, logging, mining, immigrants, homesteading, and the paper industry. Includes an exhibit on Grand Rapids native Frances Gumm, who became Judy Garland. Genealogy research center and gift shop. Open year-round.
Directions: Near the intersection of US highways 2 and 169 (N. Pokegama Avenue) in downtown Grand Rapids.

Forest History Center
2609 County Road 76, Grand Rapids, MN 55744
218-327-4482•www.mnhs.org/places/sites/fhc

What you'll find: The center tells the story of Minnesota's forests and the people who lived and worked in them more than 100 years ago.

Includes an interpretive building with exhibits and films; guided tours; a living history logging camp with costumed guides portraying a blacksmith and lumberjacks; a river barge; and a fire tower to climb. Visitor Center is open year-round.

Directions: From US Highway 169 in Grand Rapids, go west 1.8 miles on Golf Course Road to County Road 76 and turn right.

Split Rock Lighthouse
3713 Split Rock Lighthouse Road, Two Harbors, MN 55616
218-226-6372•www.mnhs.org/places/sites/srl

What you'll find: Visitors can tour the historic lighthouse, one of Minnesota's best known landmarks, which has been restored to its 1920s appearance. Split Rock Light Station was completed by the US Lighthouse Service in 1910 and it guided iron ore ships along Lake Superior until it closed in 1969. Also, tours of keeper's home, walking trails, and visitor center with exhibits and a film. Visitor center is open year-round.

Directions: About twenty miles north of Two Harbors along Minnesota Highway 61.

Comstock House Historic Site
506 Eighth Street S., Moorhead, MN 56560
218-291-4211•www.mnhs.org/places/sites/ch

What you'll find: Guided tours interpret the restored 1882 Queen Anne house and preserved original furnishings of Solomon Comstock, banker and railroad builder who helped found Moorhead State University, as well as his daughter, Ada Comstock, who became the first dean of women at the University of Minnesota and later president of Radcliffe College. Open Memorial Day Weekend through Labor Day Weekend.

Directions: From Interstate 94, take Exit 1A north on US Highway 75 (Eighth Street S.) to Fifth Avenue.

Historical & Cultural Society of Clay County
202 First Avenue N., Moorhead, MN 56560
218-299-5511 • www.hcscconline.org

What you'll find: The Hjemkomst Center museum houses and interprets the Viking ship replica Hjemkomst and its historic 1982 voyage from Duluth to Norway. Also features full-scale replica of Hopperstad Stave Church in Norway. Open year-round.
Directions: From Interstate 94, take Exit 1A north on US Highway 75 (Eighth Street S.) about two miles and turn left on N. First Avenue. Go about a half-mile to Viking Ship Park.

Hubbard County Historical Museum
301 Court Avenue, Park Rapids, MN 56470
218-732-5237 • www.rootsweb.ancestry.com/~mnhchs/

What you'll find: Hubbard County's historic courthouse has been restored and the names of the original offices still remain on the doors. Permanent exhibits include Native American artifacts, farming and logging displays, quilts, a pioneer cabin, a one-room school house, vintage clothing, and Civil War memorabilia. Open May to September.
Directions: On the corner of Third Street and Court Avenue, three blocks west of US Highway 71 in downtown Park Rapids.

Roadside Landmarks and Oddities

North West Company Fur Post
12551 Voyageur Lane, Pine City, MN 55063
320-629-6356 • www.mnhs.org/places/sites/nwcfp

What you'll find: Fifty-minute tours of recreated 1804 fur post, palisade, and lookout towers, as well as an Ojibwe encampment with seasonal demonstrations. Costumed interpreters such as a fur trade clerk bring the past to life. Visitor Center includes hands-on and interactive exhibits about the fur trade. Memorial Weekend through Labor Day Weekend; group tours by appointment year-round.
Directions: From Interstate 35 at Exit 169, one-and-a-half miles west on County Highway 7.

Willie the Walleye — Walleye Capital of the World
International Drive NE, Baudette, MN 56623
http://ci.baudette.mn.us

What you'll find: Forty-foot-long Willie the Walleye statue.
Directions: Downtown in Baudette, located south of Lake of the Woods on Minnesota highways 11 and 172.

Uncle Dan Campbell Statue
Big Falls, MN 56627
218-276-2282 • http://bigfalls.govoffice.com

What you'll find: Uncle Dan Campbell, a Scottish railroad laborer, was the first white settler in the area. Artist Terry Boquist carved the twelve-foot statue from a tree trunk.
Directions: Roadside Park (viewing of the statue) is at the intersection of US Highway 71 and Minnesota Highway 6, northeast side of Big Falls.

Paul Bunyan's Grave
Kelliher, MN 56650
218-647-8470•http://kelliher.govoffice.com

What you'll find: Headstone of Paul Bunyan.
Directions: East side of Minnesota Highway 72 (Clark Avenue S.), south of First Street SE at the Paul Bunyan Park & Campground.

Dorothy Molter Museum
2002 E. Sheridan Street, Ely, MN 55731
218-365-4451•www.rootbeerlady.com

What you'll find: The Dorothy Molter Museum is a memorial to the last resident of the Boundary Waters Canoe Area Wilderness (BWCAW). She died in 1986 after living most of her seventy-nine years on Knife Lake. Canoeists stopped at Molter's home to enjoy her famous homemade root beer. Two log cabins were transported out of the BWCAW and reassembled in Ely.
Directions: On the south side of US Highway 169 on the east end of Ely.

Soudan Underground Mine—Last and Deepest Area Mined
1379 Stuntz Bay Road, Soudan, MN 55782
218-753-2245
www.dnr.state.mn.us/state_parks/soudan_
underground_mine/index.html

What you'll find: This ninety-minute tour will take visitors a half-mile down into the earth on a cage similar to the one the miners used in earlier days. Once underground, visitors will take a three-quarter-mile train ride to the last and deepest area mined. Bring a warm coat or sweater.
Directions: Take US Highway 169 toward Ely and follow the signs.

Virginia Is Home to the Largest Loon Decoy in the World!
City Hall, 327 First Street South, Virginia, MN 55792
218-748-7535

What you'll find: The loon is twenty feet long, made of fiberglass over a metal frame, and attached to the bottom of the lake.
Directions: From US Highway 53, take the first Virginia exit and go to Silver Lake and Olcott Park parking lot for viewing of the loon on left.

Capital of American Hockey
801 Hat Trick Avenue, Eveleth, MN 55734
218-744-5167 or 800-443-7825 • www.ushockeyhall.com

What you'll find: United States Hockey Hall of Fame Museum.
Directions: Off US Highway 53 in Eveleth on Hat Trick Avenue.

World's Largest Free Standing Hockey Stick
Grant Avenue, Eveleth, MN 55734
218-744-7444 • www.evelethmn.com

What you'll find: Free-standing hockey stick weighing in at 10,000 pounds and standing 110 feet long.
Directions: Corner of Monroe Street and Grant Avenue.

Bob Dylan's Home
2425 Seventh Avenue E., Hibbing, MN 55746
www.ironrange.org/attractions/historic/dylan-home/

What you'll find: Private residence of Bob Dylan from age seven through high school, with garage door covered with a painting of Dylan's *Blood on the Tracks* album cover.
Directions: Northwest corner of Twenty-Fifth Street and Seventh Avenue East (Dylan Drive).

Hull Rust Mahoning Mine View
401 Penobscot Road, Hibbing, MN 55746
218-262-4166 • www.ironrange.org/attractions/mining

What you'll find: Largest open pit iron mine in the world.
Directions: Exit off US Highway 169 in Hibbing onto Howard Street and follow it nine blocks to Third Avenue East. Take a right and follow signs to mine.

Paul Bunyan and Babe the Blue Ox Statues
300 Bemidji Avenue, Bemidji, MN 56601
218-759-3570 • www.ci.bemidji.mn.us

What you'll find: Eighteen-foot-tall Paul Bunyan and Babe the Blue Ox statues. The second most photographed icon in the nation.
Directions: Bemidji Visitors and Convention Bureau, between Bemidji Avenue/Paul Bunyan Drive and the south shore of Lake Bemidji.

The Big Fish Supper Club
456 US Highway 2 NE, Bena, MN 56626
218-665-2299 • www.bigfishsupperclub.com

What you'll find: Photo opportunity inside the mouth of a sixty-five-foot-long tiger-stripe muskie.
Directions: North side of Highway 2, at the intersection of W. Winnie Road NE.

Judy Garland Museum
2727 US Highway 169 S., Grand Rapids, MN 55744
218-327-9276 or 800-664-JUDY
www.judygarlandmuseum.com

What you'll find: Judy Garland's memorabilia and childhood home.
Directions: West side of Highway 169 in Grand Rapids.

Split Rock Lighthouse
3713 Split Rock Lighthouse Road, Two Harbors, MN 55616
218-226-6372 • www.mnhs.org/splitrock

What you'll find: Split Rock Lighthouse has been restored and is one of America's best-preserved lighthouses.
Directions: Forty-five miles north of Duluth on Minnesota Highway 61.

Headwaters of the Mississippi River
36750 Main Park Drive, Park Rapids, MN 56470
218-699-7251 • www.dnr.state.mn.us/state_parks/itasca/index.html

What you'll find: Walk across the Mississippi River as it starts its journey 2,552 miles to the Gulf of Mexico in Itasca State Park.
Directions: South entrance to the park is twenty-three miles north of Park Rapids on US Highway 71. The north entrance is twenty-one miles south of Bagley on Minnesota highways 92 and 200.

World's Largest Tiger Muskie
Nevis City Park, Nevis, MN 56467
218-652-3866 • www.nevis.govoffice.com

What you'll find: Large fiberglass fish in a city park.
Directions: From Minnesota Highway 34, go north on Bunyan Trails Road into downtown Nevis.

Birthplace of Paul Bunyan
Broadway Street W., Akeley, MN 56433
218-652-2465 • www.akeleyminnesota.com/city.htm

What you'll find: Visitors can perch on this kneeling Paul Bunyan statue's outstretched palm.

Directions: North side of Broadway Street W. and Minnesota Highway 34.

The Statue of St. Urho, the Legendary Patron Saint of Finland

115 Second Street NE, Menahga, MN 56464

218-564-4557 • www.cityofmenahga.com

What you'll find: The statue celebrates Finnish ancestry for St. Urho Day. The Minneapolis *Star Tribune* once included St. Urho as one of the seven "must-see" tourist attractions in the state.

Directions: Located along US Highway 71 S. in Menahga.

Frank Lloyd Wright Gas Station

Corner of Cloquet Avenue and Minnesota Highway 33, Cloquet, MN 55720

218-879-1551 or 800-554-4350

www.cloquet.com/pages/community/f.l.-wright-gas-station.php

What you'll find: The R.W. Lindholm Service Station (or the Frank Lloyd Wright gas station) is the only operating gas station ever constructed from the designs of the famed architect.

Directions: From Interstate 35, take Exit 237 and go north on Highway 33 for two miles. On the southeast corner of Highway 33 and Cloquet Avenue.

Hinckley Fire Museum and Hinckley Fire Monument

106 Old Highway 61 S., Hinckley, MN 55037 (museum)

Highway 48 E., Hinckley, MN 55037 (monument)

320-384-7491 • www.hinckley.govoffice2.com

What you'll find: The Fire Museum includes dioramas, coroner's official tally, and photos of the Hinckley Fire Department. The Fire

Monument memorializes the 418 people who died in the Great Fire of 1894. Beneath it are the four trenches where 248 victims are buried. **Directions:** From Interstate 35, take Exit 183 and go west on Fire Monument Road to Old Highway 61; go right a few blocks to Fire Museum. The Fire Monument is on the east side of Interstate 35 on Minnesota Highway 48 (Fire Monument Road).

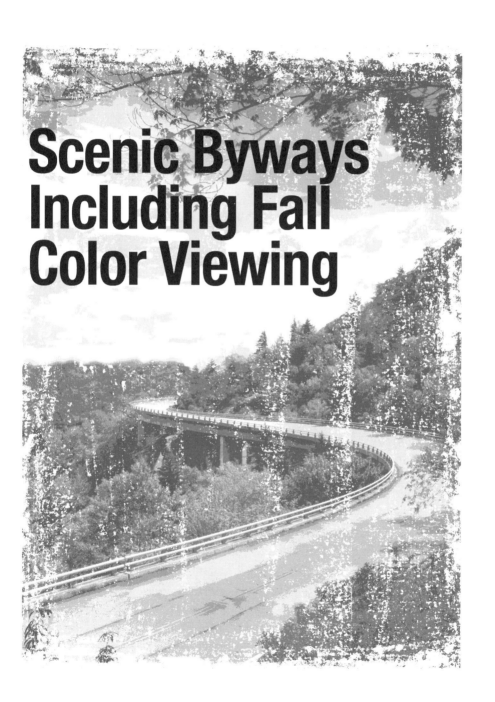

Scenic Byways Including Fall Color Viewing

Waters of the Dancing Sky Scenic Byway
Between Voyageurs National Park and the North Dakota border,
mostly on Minnesota Highway 11.
800-382-3474 • www.watersofthedancingsky.org

What you'll find: From Voyageurs National Park, along the Canadian border and all the way to North Dakota, you'll discover the rugged beauty of Minnesota's northernmost scenic drive. The 229-mile route is ideal for anglers, boaters, birders, and wildflower lovers, running along fishing favorite Rainy River from International Falls to Baudette, on from Baudette to Warroad, and along the Pine to Prairie Birding Trail west of Warroad. Zippel Bay State Park has a three-mile-long beach on the shores of Lake of the Woods. This massive lake, part of which is in Canada, is also known for its fishing. The roadside between Baudette and Warroad blooms with wildflowers, including Minnesota's state flower, the showy lady's slipper, and the area west of Warroad is part of the Pine to Prairie Birding Trail. The western end of the highway continues north on Minnesota Highway 59 to Lake Bronson State Park. Numerous resorts surround Voyageurs National Park and Lake of the Woods, two of the route's key attractions. The aurora borealis, or northern lights, frequently appear in the area thanks to its far-northern location and absence of bright city lights. Autumn colors will be at their most scenic early in the season because of the northern climate. Expect golden birch to be among the most dominant.

Gunflint Trail
County Road 12 from Grand Marais to the end of the road at
Seagull Lake.
800-338-6932 • www.gunflint-trail.com

What you'll find: Beginning in the charming harbor town of Grand Marais on Minnesota Highway 61 on Lake Superior, this paved road known as the Gunflint Trail heads up into the rolling hills of Superior

National Forest. Side roads—many of them gravel—frequently pop up and lead to resorts, campgrounds, canoe outfitters, and boat ramps. Get out your paddles, because most of the lakes are within the Boundary Waters Canoe Area Wilderness, which is mostly paddle-only. There is great fishing here and miles of hiking and cross-country skiing trails. Wildlife abounds, so there's a chance of spotting deer, moose, or bear, seeing a wide variety of birds, or hearing the howls of wolves.

Superior National Forest Scenic Byway
Follows county roads between Silver Bay, Hoyt Lakes, and Aurora.
800-777-8497
www.superiorbyways.com/superior-national-forest-scenic-byway/index.html

What you'll find: The glorious reds and yellows of hardwoods among the majesty of towering pines are some of the delights for fall color buffs along the Superior National Forest's sixty-one mile drive from Lake Superior's North Shore to the Iron Range. You won't find any towns along these county roads, but you might see migrating hawks over the Laurentian Divide at the Skibo Vista Scenic Overlook. Or you might see some of the area's other 150-plus species of birds. Other points of interest are the 1913 Toimi School, the Timber Arch Bridge, the White Pine Interpretive Trail, the Bird Lake Recreation Area, and the Cadotte Lake Recreation Area, where there is a boat landing and fishing dock.

Ladyslipper Scenic Byway
Minnesota Highway 39 between Blackduck and US Highway 2, about twenty-five miles east of Bemidji.
218-335-8600 • www.ladyslipperscenicbyway.org

What you'll find: Minnesota's state flower—actually a variety of orchid—is the namesake for this twenty-eight mile long scenic highway, which was once simply known as "Scenic Highway." The showy lady's slipper is actually uncommon in Minnesota, but flourishes along the roadsides in this region, especially north of Pennington, typically in late June. Hiking, biking, fishing, and boating are all available at Norway Beach Recreation Area on the southeast shore of Cass Lake. And if you have an interest in US history, stop at Camp Rabideau, one of only three 1930s Civilian Conservation Corps (CCC) camps in the country that are being preserved. The Blackduck area, at the north end of the byway, is the destination preferred by many hunters and anglers.

Avenue of Pines
Minnesota Highway 46 between Deer River and Northome, thirteen miles northwest of Grand Rapids.
218-335-8600 • www.byways.org/explore/byways/13551/
www.byways.org/explore/byways/13551/

What you'll find: Wander along the forty-six miles of Highway 46 and you'll see where the western prairie and northern forests meet. The road slices through the Chippewa National Forest, where red oak and white pine mingle. The area is popular for fishing, and several resorts and campgrounds are near the highway. This drive borders Lake Winnibigoshish, a favorite for fishing and known familiarly as "Lake Winnie." It is the state's fifth-largest lake, created when the Mississippi River was dammed in 1884.

Edge of the Wilderness Scenic Byway
Minnesota Highway 38 between Grand Rapids and Effie.
218-832-3161 • www.byways.org/explore/byways/2455/

What you'll find: There's a pretty good chance you'll meet a lumberjack along this stretch of the forty-seven-mile drive connecting Grand Rapids to Effie, given that it's in the heart of the Chippewa National

160

Forest and was once a vital part of the logging industry. And at the Forest History Center in Grand Rapids, a reconstructed 1900 logging camp teaches visitors about forestry and the logging industry. Highway 38 was reconstructed in recent years, promising a smooth ride through fantastic scenery where bald eagles soar over the tops of balsam fir trees. Find numerous resorts and campgrounds around Marcell, where the ranger station for the Chippewa National Forest also is located. If you're tired of driving, there are hiking trails, one of which leads to the old Joyce Estate, once a millionaire's vacation hideaway that has since fallen on hard times. Grand Rapids is home to the Judy Garland Museum as well as Judy's childhood home. Check for concerts or plays at the Myles Reif Performing Arts Center.

North Shore Scenic Drive
From Duluth to Two Harbors on Old Highway 61, and from Two Harbors to Grand Portage on Minnesota Highway 61.
800-438-5884 • www.superiorbyways.com

What you'll find: This has to be one of the most beautiful drives in the United States. As soon as you turn onto the scenic route from Duluth to Two Harbors, you'll feel the spectacular majesty of Lake Superior take over. For 154 miles, you'll see rugged shorelines, magnificent stands of forest, state parks, small towns with unique shops and galleries, and cozy restaurants that feature local fish and produce. No wonder this route has earned the national designation as an "All-American Road." There's plenty of history along with the natural beauty, too. Stop at the 1910 Split Rock Lighthouse near Gooseberry Falls, visit a commercial fishing museum in Tofte, or tour the Grand Portage National monument fur-trading post. With a theater group, art galleries, and a folk school, the harbor town of Grand Marais is an arts center. Lutsen offers a scenic golf course, a mountain-biking park, and a ski area. There's plenty to see in Duluth, a lively port city, including the Aerial Lift Bridge, Great Lakes

Aquarium, and the old Depot, home to a train museum and several arts groups. Outdoor enthusiasts will be able to appreciate up close the area's beauty and wilderness along the Superior Hiking Trail, where numerous streams and waterfalls also abound. To see Minnesota's highest waterfalls, visit Grand Portage and Tettegouche state parks.

Skyline Parkway
Follows roads overlooking Duluth.
800-438-5884
www.superiorbyways.com/duluth-skyline-parkway

What you'll find: This favorite drive of many visitors to Duluth is a thirty-six-mile route that will take you through neighborhoods and past parks from the Spirit Mountain Recreation Area to Lester Park in Duluth. It offers grand views of the city as well as of Lake Superior. A good starting point is the Thompson Hill Travel Information Center just off Interstate 35, which can provide specific driving directions. You might want to take in the beauty of Enger Park's spring daffodils and themed gardens, or climb the five-story Enger Tower for a view of Duluth and Superior, Wis. — the Twin Ports. If you're a hiker, you may want to stroll the trails at Lester Park or the rugged, two-mile backwoods trail at Chester Park. Hawk Ridge Nature Reserve is popular with birders.

Rushing Rapids Parkway
Minnesota Highway 210 from Carlton to the Fond du Lac neighborhood in southwest Duluth.
http://minnesotascenicbyways.com/rushingRapidsParkway.html

What you'll find: Short, but sweet — that describes the Rushing Rapids Parkway at only nine miles long. The route cuts a path through beautiful hardwood forests and walls of slate in Jay Cooke State Park, highlighted each spring with wildflowers and each fall with abundant autumn color. The route meets the northern tip of the Veterans Evergreen Memorial Drive, and the sixty-three mile paved Willard Munger Bike Trail passes through the park. There are fifty miles of hiking trails along the St. Louis River and throughout the hills.

Veterans Evergreen Memorial Scenic Byway
Minnesota Highway 23 between Interstate 35 west of Askov to Duluth.
http://minnesotascenicbyways.com/veteransEvergreenMemorial.html

What you'll find: Veterans Evergreen Memorial Scenic Byway is a beautiful country road between Jay Cooke and Banning state parks, and known to be the "scenic route" to Duluth. The fifty-mile byway is dedicated to World War I and World War II soldiers from nearby counties (complete with memorial plaques), and is an excellent spot to view glorious fall colors in the St. Louis River Valley. Trout fishing is said to be excellent here, especially on the Nemadji and South Fork rivers.

Lake Country Scenic Byway
Minnesota Highway 34 between Detroit Lakes and Walker, and north from Park Rapids to Itasca State Park on US Highway 71.
800-247-0054 • www.lakecountryscenicbyway.com

What you'll find: Sure, you can stride across the Mississippi River at the headwaters in Itasca State Park, but there are plenty of other attractions along this eighty-eight-mile drive. The Lake Country Scenic Byway follows part of Minnesota's Pine to Prairie Birding Trail, and also connects three "anchor" towns: Walker, Park Rapids, and Detroit Lakes. There are miles of hiking and biking trails, art galleries, music festivals, and roadside diners, along with lodges, resorts, golf courses, and birdwatching opportunities (especially at Itasca and the Tamarac National Wildlife Refuge).

King of Trails Scenic Byway

US Highway 75 near the western border of the state, running the
entire length of Minnesota.

800-336-6125 • www.highway75.com

What you'll find: To follow the 414-mile Minnesota stretch of the
International Historic Highway 75 King of Trails Scenic Byway is to
follow in the footsteps of Minnesota's native peoples. Pipestone
National Monument in southwestern Minnesota preserves the area
where, for centuries, Indians have quarried the rock used in peace pipes.
Nearby, you will find a buffalo herd grazing at Blue Mounds State Park
and fields of wind turbines along Buffalo Ridge near Lake Benton.
Crops of corn and soybeans change to potatoes and beets on a
northbound drive. With five state parks spread out along the way, the
King of Trails is a bird lover's paradise. The Minnesota River begins
twisting its way across the state from Big Stone Lake State Park, and the
Big Stone National Wildlife Refuge is a good stop for birders. Pipestone
and Crookston boast some elegant nineteenth-century homes along the
route, and Moorhead, the largest city on the route, is home to the
Hjemkomst Center, the Comstock House, and several arts
organizations.

Tours and Excursions

Polaris Experience Center and Factory Tour
205 Fifth Avenue SW, Suite 2, Roseau, MN 56751
218-463-4999•www.polarisindustries.com/en-us/OurCompany/
AboutPolaris/Pages/PolarisExperienceCenter.aspx

What you'll find: The 5,600-square-foot Experience Center has displays, photographs, videos, and memorabilia about the company known for snowmobiles and all-terrain vehicles. Gift shop. In addition, there are daily tours for the nearby main plant where visitors can watch snowmobiles and ATVs being built.
Directions: In Roseau along Minnesota Highway 89.

Boise Paper Solutions Mill Tours
400 Second Street, International Falls, MN 56649
218-285-5011•www.rainylake.org/thingstodo.html

What you'll find: View one of world's largest and fastest paper-making machines on this free tour. Ranked as one of the top such tours in the country by *Touring America Magazine.* June through August or by reservation.
Directions: From the junction of US highways 71 and 53, go one block north and one block west.

Rainy Lake Boat Tours
Rainy and Kabetogama lakes, International Falls, MN 56649
888-381-2873 or 218-286-5258
www.nps.gov/voya/planyourvisit/rainyboattours.htm

What you'll find: Guided boat tours in Voyageurs National Park in the summer; visitors can watch wildlife, boat to the historic Kettle Falls Hotel, and hike around the gold mines on Little American Island.

Directions: Depart from Rainy Lake Visitor Center, about twelve miles east of International Falls off Minnesota Highway 11, turn right on County Road 96 (Park Road). Or depart from Kabetogama Lake Visitor Center, about twenty-five miles south of International Falls; turn off US Highway 53 onto County Highway 122.

Burntside Heritage Tours
Burntside Lodge
2755 Burntside Lodge Road, Ely, MN 55731
218-365-5445 • http://burntsidetours.com

What you'll find: Pontoon boat cruise on Burntside Lake includes retracing early logging activities, learning geological history, and seeing some original summer homes, naturalist Sigurd Olson's Listening Point, the historic Burntside Lodge, the sunken boat Bull of the Woods, and Indian Island. Runs June through September.
Directions: About six miles northwest of Ely via US Highway 169 and Minnesota Highway 1. Turn north on Grant McMahan Boulevard and left at Burntside Lodge Road (County Road 489).

Grand Portage-Isle Royale Transportation Line, Inc.
Hat Point Marina, 402 Upper Road, Grand Portage, MN 55605
218-475-0024 or 651-653-5872 or 888-746-2305
www.isleroyaleboats.com/daytrips.asp

What you'll find: Go by boat to Isle Royale National Park on Lake Superior, May through September. Tour includes viewing of the little Spirit Cedar Tree, the Suzie Islands, the sunken steamship *America*, the Rock of Ages Light House, Washington Harbor, and Windigo. On day trips, visitors get four hours on the island for guided hikes, picnics, or relaxing.

Directions: From Minnesota Highway 61, turn right at Stevens Road, take the first right onto County Road 73 (Store Road), turn left at County Road 17 (Mile Creek Road), then right at Bay Road and right again at County Road 17 (Upper Road) to marina.

Agassiz Environmental Learning Center
400 Summit Avenue SW, Fertile, MN 56540
218-945-3129 • www.aelcfertile.org

What you'll find: A nature center that offers an outdoor classroom and recreation in the Fertile Sand Hills. The center covers 640 acres and has sand dunes, oak savanna, dry sand prairie, and lowland forests. Includes more than ten miles of hiking and cross-country ski trails, a campground, and a deck overlooking the Sand Hill River.
Directions: From Minnesota Highway 32 in Fertile, turn west on Summit Avenue SW.

Coborn's Lake Itasca Tours, Inc.
54725 Sunset Street, Itasca State Park, Osage, MN 56570
218-266-3660 or 218-573-2216 (off-season) • www.lakeitascatours.com

What you'll find: Daily narrated two-hour naturalist tours on the Chester Charles II follow the route of Ozawindib when he guided Henry Rowe Schoolcraft to the Mississippi Headwaters on Lake Itasca in 1832. Also dinner buffet cruises, sunset cruises, and private charters. Enjoy history, wildlife, and nature photography. Runs from Memorial Weekend to Labor Day with limited September schedule.
Directions: In Itasca State Park at Douglas Lodge pier, off US Highway 71 about twenty miles north of Park Rapids.

Blandin Paper Mill Tours
115 SW First Street, Grand Rapids, MN 55744
218-327-6682
www.visitgrandrapids.com/vacations/attractions/attractions_02.html

What you'll find: Free guided tour of the mill June through Labor Day includes a video that follows the process of making paper from cutting down the tree to seeing the finished product. No children under 12.

Directions: From US Highway 2 in Grand Rapids, go south a few blocks on Highway 169, then west on SW First Street.

Hill Annex Mine Tour
880 Gary Street, Calumet, MN 55716
218-247-7215•www.dnr.state.mn.us/state_parks/hill_annex_mine

What you'll find: A one-and-a-half hour bus tour that retraces the route miners took for sixty years to get to their jobs in this open-pit, natural iron ore mine. Tour stops include the operations area and huge vintage equipment. A separate fossil-hunting tour is also offered. Memorial Weekend through Labor Day.

Directions: From US Highway 169 in Calumet, go north on Gary Street about five blocks to the end of the street.

Hull Rust Mahoning Mine Tour
401 Penobscot Road, Hibbing, MN 55746
218-262-4166 or 218-262-4900•www.ironrange.org/attractions/mining

What you'll find: View a working mine from observation area in Hibbing, the world's largest open pit iron ore mine, a national historic landmark. Open mid-May through September.

Directions: Exit off US Highway 169 in Hibbing onto Howard Street and follow it nine blocks to Third Avenue East. Take a right and follow signs to mine.

Tofte Charters
Tofte, MN 55615
218-663-9932 or 866-663-9932•www.toftecharters.com

What you'll find: Sightseeing cruises or fishing trips on Lake Superior with views of the Sawtooth Mountains and the Superior National Forest. Lake trout are caught year-round; other species caught include king (Chinook), coho, and pink salmon, as well as steelhead.
Directions: Depart from Taconite Harbor, six miles south of Tofte off Minnesota Highway 61.

MudPaw ATV Adventures
68 Hays Circle, Suite 4 (mailing address), Silver Bay, MN 55614
218-220-0415•www.mudpawatv.com

What you'll find: One-hour or half-day guided tours on all-terrain vehicles on trails along Lake Superior's North Shore. Scenery includes lakes, cliffs, rivers, gorges, and Lake Superior.
Directions: From Minnesota Highway 61 at Silver Bay, turn left onto Outer Drive and proceed two miles through town and past the four-way stop to the Penn Boulevard parking area on the right.

Amicus Adventure Sailing
133 Third Avenue, Two Harbors, MN 55616
218-290-5975•www.amicusadventuresailing.com

What you'll find: Family, individual and group chartered sailing trips from two hours to two weeks on Lake Superior to the North Shore, Apostle Islands, and Isle Royale.

Directions: From Scenic North Shore Drive (Old Highway 61) between Duluth and Two Harbors, go south to Knife River and turn toward Lake Superior on Marina Drive to the Knife River Marina.

Sport Trolling, Inc.
Two Harbors, MN 55616
218-830-1050 or 218-834-4270 • www.fishduluth.com/rainbowsend

What you'll find: Chartered fishing trips on the thirty-seven-foot Rainbow's End from the Knife River and Silver Bay marinas on Lake Superior. Specialty is following the salmon migration. Afternoon sightseeing cruises available.

Directions: From Scenic North Shore Drive (Old Highway 61) between Duluth and Two Harbors, go south to Knife River and turn toward Lake Superior on Marina Drive to the Knife River Marina.

Carriage House Charters
1204 Lake Avenue S., Duluth, MN 55802
218-260-9595 or 218-727-1052 • www.carriagehousecharters.com

What you'll find: Half-day or full-day sailboat rides on Lake Superior and Superior Bay. Itineraries may include a cruise along the North Shore; a route from Duluth out under the Aerial Lift Bridge and over to Superior, Wisconsin; or a harbor cruise to view grain elevators, iron ore and coal docks, and ships and tugs.

Directions: From Interstate 35 in Duluth, take Exit 256B (Fifth Avenue W./Lake Avenue) and go across the Aerial Lift Bridge on Lake Avenue onto Park Point.

Lake Superior Brewing Company
2711 W. Superior Street, Duluth, MN 55806
218-723-4000•http://lakesuperiorbrewing.com

What you'll find: Tours are available at Duluth's only microbrewery, which started in the early 1990s, and brews four beers year-round: Special Ale, Kayak Kolsch, Mesabi Red, and Sir Duluth Oatmeal Stout. Seasonal varieties include Split Rock Bock, Windward Wheat, St. Louis Bay IPA, and Old Man Winter Warmer.
Directions: From Interstate 35 in Duluth, take Exit 254 and go inland on S. Twenty-Seventh Avenue W. to Superior Street and turn left.

Lake Superior Sportfishing Charters
5147 Lester River Road, Duluth, MN 55804
218-390-4522•www.lakesuperiorfishing.com

What you'll find: Charter fishing on Lake Superior for salmon, lake trout, and walleye.
Directions: From Interstate 35 in Duluth, take Exit 256B (Fifth Avenue W./Lake Avenue). Moored at the Waterfront Plaza Marina halfway down the length of the *S.S. William A. Irvin* ore boat.

North Shore Scenic Railroad
506 W. Michigan Street, Duluth, MN 55802
218-722-1273 or 800-423-1273•www.northshorescenicrailroad.org

What you'll find: During the summer, several trains a day depart from the historical Union Depot for trips to Two Harbors or the Lester River. Specialty trips include pizza train, murder mystery, fall colors, and birthday parties. Narrated tours tell the history of Duluth, its harbor, and its railroads.

172

Directions: From Interstate 35 in Duluth, take Exit 256A (Mesaba Avenue) toward Superior Street, then turn slight right onto W. Michigan Street.

Port Town Trolley–Duluth Transit Authority
2402 W. Michigan Street, Duluth, MN 55806
218-722-7283 • www.duluthtransit.com/riderguide/porttowntrolley.aspx

What you'll find: The Port Town Trolley circulates daily in summer among downtown Duluth, Canal Park, and Bayfront Park every thirty minutes, serving hotels, restaurants, shops, and tourist attractions.
Directions: Find trolley stops along Canal Park Drive, on Superior Street, and along the Bayfront in downtown Duluth.

S.S. William A. Irvin Guided Tours
350 Harbor Drive, Duluth, MN 55802
218-722-7876 (in season) or 218-727-0022, ext. 234 (off-season)
www.decc.org/omnimax-irvin/william-a-irvin.html

What you'll find: Sixty-minute guided tour on the 610-foot flagship of US Steel's Great Lakes Fleet that carried iron ore from 1937 to 1978. Guests of the company traveled in style with luxury cabins trimmed in oak and walnut with brass railings. May through September and haunted ship tours in October.
Directions: Just off Interstate 35 at Exit 256B (Fifth Avenue W./Lake Avenue), docked next to the Duluth Entertainment Convention Center.

Vista Fleet Harbor Cruises
323 Harbor Drive, Duluth, MN 55802
218-722-6218 or 877-883-4002 • http://vistafleet.com

What you'll find: Daily sightseeing cruises, sunset dinner cruises, family pizza cruises, and private events on Lake Superior and in the Duluth-Superior Harbor from May into October.
Directions: Just off Interstate 35 at Exit 256B (Fifth Avenue W./Lake Avenue) and take Harbor Drive to the harbor side of the Duluth Entertainment Convention Center.

Snake River Outfitters of Minnesota
21406 Aubrecht Shores Drive, Pine City, MN 55063
303-435-6726 or 612-718-0125 • www.snakeriveroutfittersmn.com

What you'll find: Canoe and kayak rental for small or large groups of people with shuttle and choice of drop-off points. Guided fishing, sunset, and pizza canoe trips, and tours in a large voyageur canoe to the Northwest Company Fur Post. Campsites and box lunches available. May to September.
Directions: From Interstate 35, take exit 169 onto County Highway 7 (Hillside Avenue), then left on Main Street/Sixth Street SW and go about eight-tenths of a mile, turn right.

Breweries
and Wineries

Two Fools Vineyard
12501 240th Avenue SE, Plummer, MN 56748
218-465-4655 • www.twofoolsvineyard.com

Open: Late June to September
What you'll find: Fertile soil and long summer days are behind the rich flavor in the berries and grapes grown at Two Fools Vineyard, Minnesota's northernmost vineyard. LeRoy and Carol Stumpf took their hobby and a few grapevines and now use the fruit of those vines as well as other fruits, berries, and rhubarb raised on their property and from other grape-producing regions to make their specialty wines. Red, white, and fruit wines are available and are likely to be offered at weekend tastings.
Directions: About 13.5 miles southeast of Thief River Falls: seven miles south on US Highway 59, then four miles east on Country Road 3 (Center Street E.), then two-and-a-half miles south on 240th Avenue SE.

Lake Superior Brewing Company
2711 W. Superior Street, Duluth, MN 55806
218-723-4000 • http://lakesuperiorbrewing.com

Open: Year-round
What you'll find: Duluth's only microbrewery started in the early 1990s when a local scientist lost his job and decided to pursue his dream. With the help of friends and other craft brewers, Lake Superior Brewing grew, and while the business changed hands, the innovative spirit remained. You can always expect to find four beers year-round at Lake Superior Brewing Company: Special Ale, Kayak Kolsch, Mesabi Red, and Sir Duluth Oatmeal Stout. Seasonal varieties include Split Rock Bock, Windward Wheat, St. Louis Bay IPA, and Old Man Winter Warmer. Tours are available.
Directions: From Interstate 35 in Duluth, take Exit 254 and go inland on S. Twenty-Seventh Avenue W. to Superior Street and turn left.

Forestedge Winery

35295 Minnesota Highway 64, Laporte, MN 56461
218-224-3535 • www.forestedgewinery.com

Open: Early May to late December

What you'll find: Tucked away from main roads, Forestedge Winery produces light, dry wines from strawberries, chokecherries, raspberries, plums, and other fruits grown locally in this northern Minnesota resort region. Rhubarb wine is Forestedge's specialty and has won awards for its crisp, clean taste. Visitors can explore the area on winding nature paths, see the gardens where the fruit and berries are grown, visit with the winemakers, tour the production area, and kick back in the bistro area, tasting the final product. Stop at the gift shop for wooden cooking tools and other items created by artisans from around the country.

Directions: About five miles southwest of Laporte on Highway 64 via Minnesota Highway 200, or about twenty-five miles south of Bemidji.

Leech Lake Brewing Company

195 Walker Industries Boulevard, Walker, MN 56484
218-547-4746 • www.leechlakebrewing.com

Open: Year-round, but check the website or call for hours.

What you'll find: Greg and Gina Smith opened the brewery in 2010. Greg, a home brewer since 1992, had dreamed of opening his own brewing company, and the dream took shape when the couple moved from Colorado to Walker. Leech Lake Brewing Company, located near the shores of Leech Lake, specializes in keg- and bottle-conditioned British-style ales, including the staples: Loch Leech Monster Scottish Ale, Blindside Pale Ale, 47° North India Pale Ale, Minobii ESB, Driven Snow Robust Porter, and 3 Sheets Imperial India Pale Ale.

Directions: In Walker, take Minnesota highways 200 and 371 (Minnesota Avenue W.) west to Sautbine Road NW and turn left; take second left onto Town Hall Road NW.

Restaurants and Cafés

WARROAD

Arnesen's Rocky Point Resort
6760 Rocky Point Road NW, Roosevelt, MN 56673
218-442-7215•www.arnesens.com/lodge_dining.html

What you'll find: American food.

Daisy Garden Restaurant
115 Wabasha Avenue NE, Warroad, MN 56763
218-386-1763•www.daisygardenrestaurant.com

What you'll find: American and Chinese food.

Lakeview Restaurant
1205 Lake Street NE, Warroad, MN 56763
218-386-1225•www.sevenclanscasino.com

What you'll find: American food.

M & K Takeouts
209 State Avenue SW, Warroad, MN 56763
218-386-3335•www.marnie.com/MKT

What you'll find: Assorted fast food.

Main Street Bar & Grill
118 Main Avenue NE, Warroad, MN 56763
218-386-9955

What you'll find: American food.

Patch Restaurant
701 N. State Avenue, Warroad, MN 56763
218-386-2082

What you'll find: American and Mexican food.

INTERNATIONAL FALLS

Border Bar Pizza Parlor
415 Third Avenue, International Falls, MN 56649
218-283-2222

What you'll find: Pizza and American food.

Chocolate Moose Restaurant Company
2501 Second Avenue W., International Falls, MN 56649
218-283-8888 • www.chocolatemooserestaurant.com

What you'll find: American food.

Giovanni's Pizza
301 Third Avenue, International Falls, MN 56649
218-283-2600 • www.giosifalls.com/menu.html

What you'll find: Italian and American food.

Margarita's Mexican Grill
1323 Third Street, International Falls, MN 56649
218-283-3333

What you'll find: Mexican food.

Rose Garden Restaurant
311 Fourth Avenue, International Falls, MN 56649
218-283-4551

What you'll find: Chinese food.

Sandy's Place
1510 Second Avenue, International Falls, MN 56649
218-285-9108

What you'll find: American food.

THIEF RIVER FALLS

China King Restaurant
304 Third Street E., Thief River Falls, MN 56701
218-681-3858

What you'll find: Chinese food.

Evergreen Eating
700 Minnesota Highway 32 S., Thief River Falls, MN 56701
218-681-3138 • www.evergreeneating.com

What you'll find: American food.

Lantern Restaurant & Lounge
1910 US Highway 59 S., Thief River Falls, MN 56701
218-681-8211

What you'll find: American food.

South China Buffet
123 Third Street W., Thief River Falls, MN 56701
218-681-8880

What you'll find: Chinese food.

CROOKSTON

China Moon
114 S. Broadway, Crookston, MN 56716
218-281-3136

What you'll find: Chinese food.

El Metate Authentic Mexican
2315 N. Acres Drive, Crookston, MN 56716
218-281-3375

What you'll find: Mexican food.

Happy Joe's Pizza & Ice Cream
705 E. Robert Street, Crookston, MN 56716
218-281-5141•www.happyjoes.com

What you'll find: Pizza and ice cream.

The Irishman's Shanty
1501 S. Main, Crookston, MN 56716
218-281-9912•www.irishmansshanty.com

What you'll find: American food.

ELY

Blue Heron
827 Kawishiwi Trail, Ely, MN 55731
218-365-4740•www.blueheronbnb.com

What you'll find: American food.

Britton's Café
5 E. Chapman Street, Ely, MN 55731
218-365-3195

What you'll find: American food.

Burntside Lodge
2755 Burntside Lodge Road, Ely, MN 55731
218-365-3894•www.burntside.com

What you'll find: American food.

Cranberry's Restaurant and Saloon
47 E. Sheridan Street, Ely, MN 55731
218-365-4301

What you'll find: American food.

Ely Steakhouse
216 E. Sheridan, Ely, MN 55731
218-365-7412•www.elysteakhouse.com

What you'll find: American food.

Silver Rapids Lodge
459 Kawishiwi Trail, Ely, MN 55731
218-365-4877 • silverrapidslodge.com

What you'll find: American food.

VIRGINIA

Jues Chinese Restaurant & Lounge
312 Chestnut Street, Virginia, MN 55792
218-741-7695

What you'll find: Chinese food.

La Cocina & Cantina
407 Chestnut Street, Virginia, MN 55792
218-749-8226

What you'll find: Mexican food.

Saigon Café
111 N. Second Avenue, Virginia, MN 55792
218-741-6465

What you'll find: Vietnamese food.

The Sawmill
5478 Mountain Iron Drive, Virginia, MN 55792
218-741-8681 • www.sawmillsaloonrestaurant.com

What you'll find: Pizza and sandwiches.

GRAND MARAIS

Blue Water Café
20 W. Wisconsin Street, Grand Marais, MN 55604
218-387-1597

What you'll find: American food.

Chez Jude Restaurant & Wine Café
411 W. Minnesota Highway 61, Grand Marais, MN 55604
218-387-9113 • www.chezjude.com

What you'll find: American (contemporary Minnesota cuisine).

The Crooked Spoon Café
17 W. Wisconsin Street, Grand Marais, MN 55604
218-387-2779 • www.crookedspooncafe.com

What you'll find: American food.

My Sister's Place
401 E. Minnesota Highway 61, Grand Marais, MN 55604
218-387-1915 • www.mysistersplacerestaurant.com

What you'll find: American food.

The Naniboujou Lodge and Restaurant
20 Naniboujou Trail, Grand Marais, MN 55604
218-387-2688

What you'll find: American food.

The Pie Place
2017 W. Minnesota Highway 61, Grand Marais, MN 55604
218-387-1513•www.northshorepieplace.com

What you'll find: American food (homemade North Woods cuisine).

South of the Border Café
4 W. Minnesota Highway 61, Grand Marais, MN 55604
218-387-1505

What you'll find: American food (breakfasts, burgers, and fries).

Sven & Ole's
9 W. Wisconsin Street, Grand Marais, MN 55604
218-387-1713•www.svenandoles.com

What you'll find: Pizza.

LUTSEN

Cascade Lodge & Restaurant
3719 W. Minnesota Highway 61, Lutsen, MN 55612
218-387-1112•www.cascadelodgemn.com

What you'll find: American food.

Lutsen Resort
5700 W. Minnesota Highway 61, Lutsen, MN 55612
218-663-7212•www.lutsenresort.com/dining

What you'll find: American food.

Moguls Grille and Tap Room
377 Ski Hill Road, Lutsen, MN 55612
218-663-3020 • www.caribouhighlands.com

What you'll find: American food.

Papa Charlie's Tavern & Stage
476 Ski Hill Road, Lutsen, MN 55612
218-663-7800 • www.lutsen.com

What you'll find: American food.

Poplar River Pub
5700 W. Minnesota Highway 61, Lutsen, MN 55612
218-663-7212 • www.lutsenresort.com

What you'll find: American food.

Rosie's Café
452 Ski Hill Road, Lutsen, MN 55612
218-663-7281

What you'll find: Breakfast and lunch (during ski season).

Summit Chalet
445 Ski Hill Road, Lutsen, MN 55612
218-663-7281

What you'll find: American food (lunch cafeteria style).

TOFTE

Bluefin Bay
7192 W. Minnesota Highway 61, Tofte, MN 55615
218-663-7296•www.bluefinbay.com

What you'll find: American food.

Coho Café & Bakery
7126 W. Minnesota Highway 61, Tofte, MN 55615
218-663-8032•www.bluefinbay.com

What'll you'll find: American food.

SILVER BAY

Bri-Esa's Deli
94 Outer Drive, Silver Bay, MN 55614
218-226–4694

What you'll find: American food (sub sandwiches and pizza).

Jimmy's Pizza
96 Outer Drive, Silver Bay, MN 55614
218-226-4241•www.jimmyspizza.com

What you'll find: Pizza.

Northwood Café
Shopping Center No. 6, Silver Bay, MN 55614
218-226-3699

What'll you'll find: American food.

BEAVER BAY

Blue Anchor
1012 Main Street, Beaver Bay, MN 55601
218-226-3221

What you'll find: American food.

Cove Point Crossings Bar & Grill
4614 Minnesota Highway 61, Beaver Bay, MN 55601
218-226–4036•www.covepointlodge.com

What you'll find: American food (pizzas, salads, gourmet sandwiches, and wraps).

Cove Point Lodge
4614 Minnesota Highway 61, Beaver Bay, MN 55601
218-226-3221•www.covepointlodge.com

What you'll find: American food (dinner only).

Lemon Wolf Café
605 Town Road, Beaver Bay, MN 55601
218-226–7225•www.lemonwolfcafe.com

What you'll find: American food.

Northern Lights Roadhouse
1040 Main Street, Beaver Bay, MN 55601
218-226-3012•www.northernlightsroadhouse-pub.com

What you'll find: American and Scandinavian food.

FINLAND

Our Place
5195 Heffelfinger Road, Finland, MN 55603
218-353–7343

What you'll find: American food.

Tressel Inn
9459 County Road 7, Cramer Road, Finland, MN 55603
218-830-0523•www.trestleinn.com

What you'll find: American food (known for burgers).

West Branch Bar and Grill
6701 Minnesota Highway 1, Finland, MN 55603
218-353-7493

What you'll find: American food.

TWO HARBORS

Betty's Pies
1633 Minnesota Highway 61, Two Harbors, MN 55616
218-834-3367 or 877-269-7494•www.bettyspies.com

What you'll find: American food (burgers, wraps, salad, and pies).

Black Woods Wood-Fired Grill & Bar
612 Seventh Avenue, Two Harbors, MN 55616
218-834-3846•www.blackwoods.com

What you'll find: American food.

Dixie Bar & Grill
2505 Minnesota Highway 2, Two Harbors, MN 55616
218-834-2846•www.dixiebarandgrill.com

What you'll find: American food.

DO North Pizza
15 County Highway 20, Two Harbors, MN 55616
218-834-3555•www.donorthpizza.com

What you'll find: Pizza.

Judy's Café
623 Seventh Avenue, Two Harbors, MN 55616
218-834-4802

What you'll find: American food.

Kamloops Restaurant
1521 Superior Shores Drive, Two Harbors, MN 55616
218-834-5671 • www.superiorshores.com

What you'll find: American food.

Vanilla Bean Café
812 Seventh Avenue, Two Harbors, MN 55616
218-834-3714 • www.thevanillabean.com

What you'll find: American food.

DULUTH

Amazing Grace Bakery & Café
394 Lake Avenue S., Duluth, MN 55802
218-723-0075 • www.amazinggracebakeryduluth.com

What you'll find: Soup and sandwiches.

Bellisio's Italian Restaurant
400 Lake Avenue S., Duluth, MN 55802
218-727-4921 • www.grandmasrestaurants.com

What you'll find: Italian food.

Burrito Union
1332 E. Fourth Street, Duluth, MN 55802
218-728-4414 • www.burritounion.com

What you'll find: Mexican food.

Chester Creek Café At Sara's Table
1902 E. Eighth Street, Duluth, MN 55812
218-724-6811•www.astccc.net

What you'll find: Vegetarian food.

Famous Dave's
355 Lake Avenue S., Duluth, MN 55802
218-740-3180•www.famousdaves.com/duluth

What you'll find: American food (barbeque).

Fitger's Brewhouse Brewery and Grille
600 E. Superior Street, Duluth, MN 55802
218-279-2739•www.fitgers.com

What you'll find: American (pub fare) and handcrafted beer.

Grandma's Restaurants
522 Lake Avenue S., Duluth, MN 55802
2202 Maple Grove Road, Duluth, MN 55811
218-727-4192 and 218-722-9313•www.grandmasrestaurants.com

What you'll find: American food.

Green Mill Restaurant
340 Lake Avenue S., Duluth, MN 55802
218-727-7000•www.greenmill.com

What you'll find: Pizza and American food.

Hanabi Japanese Cuisine
110 N. First Avenue W., Duluth, MN 55802
218-464-4412•www.hanabimn.com

What you'll find: Japanese food.

JJ Astor Restaurant
505 W. Superior Street, Floor 16 (Radisson Hotel), Duluth, MN 55802
218-727-8981•www.jjastorrestaurant.com

What you'll find: American food.

Lake Avenue Restaurant & Bar
394 Lake Avenue S., Duluth, MN 55802
218-722-2355•www.lakeavenuecafe.com

What you'll find: Eclectic food (American, European).

Lighthouse on Homestead
5730 Homestead Road, Duluth, MN 55804
218-525-4525•www.lighthouseonhomestead.com

What you'll find: American food.

Midi Restaurant
600 E. Superior Street, Duluth, MN 55802
218-727-4880•www.midirestaurant.net

What you'll find: Mediterranean food.

New Scenic Café
5461 North Shore Drive, Duluth, MN 55804
218-525-6274 • www.newsceniccafe.com

What you'll find: American food.

Nokomis Restaurant
5593 North Shore Drive, Duluth, MN 55804
218-525-2286 • www.nokomisonthelake.com

What you'll find: American food.

Pickwick Restaurant & Pub
508 E. Superior Street, Duluth, MN 55802
218-623-7425 • www.pickwickduluth.com

What you'll find: American food (steaks and fish).

Pizza Lucé
11 E. Superior Street, Duluth, MN 55802
218-727-7400 • www.pizzaluce.com

What you'll find: Pizza.

Porter's Restaurant
207 W. Superior Street, Duluth, MN 55802
218-727-6746 • www.hiduluth.com

What you'll find: American food.

Restaurant 301
301 E. Superior Street, Duluth, MN 55802
218-733-5660 or 888-627-8122•www.sheraton.com/Duluth

What you'll find: American food.

Texas Roadhouse
902 Mall Drive, Duluth, MN 55811
218-624-7427•www.texasroadhouse.com

What you'll find: American food (steaks/ribs).

Thai Krathong Restaurant
308 Lake Avenue S., Duluth, MN 55802
218-733-9774•www.thaikrathongduluth.com

What you'll find: Thai food.

Va Bene Berarducci's Caffe
734 E. Superior Street, Duluth, MN 55802
218-722-1518•www.vabenecaffe.com

What you'll find: Italian food.

Valentini's Vicino Lago
1400 London Road, Duluth, MN 55805
218-728-5900•www.valentinisduluth.com

What you'll find: Italian food.

BEMIDJI

Brigid's Cross Irish Pub
317 Beltrami Avenue NW, Bemidji, MN 56601
218-444-0567•www.brigidsirishpub.com

What you'll find: Irish food.

Cabin Coffee House & Café
214 Third Street Northwest, Bemidji, MN 56601
218-444-2899•www.cabincoffeehouse.com

What you'll find: Sandwiches and wraps.

Dave's Pizza
422 Fifteenth Street NW, Bemidji, MN 56601
218-751-3225•www.davespizza.biz

What you'll find: Pizza.

Keith's Old River Pizza Company
1425 Paul Bunyan Drive NW, Bemidji, MN 56601
218-751-7941•www.keithspizza.com

What you'll find: Pizza.

Peppercorn Restaurant
1813 Paul Bunyan Drive NW, Bemidji, MN 56601
218-759-2794•www.peppercornrestaurant.com

What you'll find: American food.

Tutto Bene
300 Beltrami Avenue NW, Bemidji, MN 56601
218-751-1100

What you'll find: Italian food.

SIDE LAKE

Bimbo's Octagon
7686 County Road 5, Side Lake, MN 55781
218-254-2576

What you'll find: Pizza.

Ciao! Rustic Italian
12860 Rudstrom Road, Side Lake, MN 55781
218-254-2007 • www.ciaorusticitalian.com

What you'll find: Wood-fire pizza and pasta.

HIBBING

Brick Yard Bar & Restaurant
408 E. Howard Street, Hibbing, MN 55746
218-263-5298 • www.brickyardhibbing.com

What you'll find: American food.

China Buffet
102 E. Howard Street, Hibbing, MN 55746
218-263-6324

What you'll find: Chinese food.

Grandma's in the Park
1402 E. Howard Street, Hibbing, MN 55746
218-262-3481 • www.hibbingparkhotel.com

What you'll find: American food.

The Pizza Ranch Restaurant
2502 E. Beltline, Hibbing, MN 55746
218-262-0085 • www.pizzaranch.com

What you'll find: Pizza.

Sammy's Pizza & Restaurant
106 E. Howard Street, Hibbing, MN 55746
218-263-7574 • www.mysammys.com

What you'll find: Pizza and Italian food.

Sportsmen's Restaurant
509 E. Howard Street, Hibbing, MN 55746
218-262-2714

What you'll find: American food.

Zimmy's Restaurant
531 E. Howard Street, Hibbing, MN 55746
218-262-6145•www.zimmys.com

What you'll find: American food and Bob Dylan memorabilia.

NASHWAUK

Wizard's Bar & Grill
102 Central Avenue, Nashwauk, MN 55769
218-885-3080

What you'll find: Bar food.

GRAND RAPIDS

17th Street Grill
144 SE Seventeenth Street, Grand Rapids, MN 55744
218-326-2600•www.timberlakelodgehotel.com

What you'll find: American food.

Cedars Dining Room
2301 S. US Highway 169, Grand Rapids, MN 55744
218-326-8501•www.sawmillinn.com

What you'll find: American food.

El Potro Mexican Restaurant
510 S. Pokegama Avenue, Grand Rapids, MN 55744
218-326-6275

What you'll find: Mexican food.

Forest Lake Restaurant
1201 NW Fourth Street, Grand Rapids, MN 55744
218-326-3423 • www.forestlakerestaurant.com

What you'll find: American food.

Sammy's Pizza & Restaurant
802 S. Pokegama Avenue, Grand Rapids, MN 55744
218-326-8551 • www.mysammys.com

What you'll find: Pizza and pasta.

Zorbaz on the Lake
32946 Crystal Springs Road, Grand Rapids, MN 55744
218-326-1006 • www.zorbaz.com

What you'll find: Pizza and Mexican food.

COHASSET

Jack's Bar and Grill
37584 Otis Lane, Cohasset, MN 55721
218-327-1462 • www.sugarlakelodge.com

What you'll find: American food.

Otis's Restaurant
37584 Otis Lane, Cohasset, MN 55721
218-327-1462

What you'll find: American food.

MOORHEAD

Erbert & Gerbert's
212 S. Eighth Street, Moorhead, MN 56560
218-287-7827•www.erbertandgerberts.com

What you'll find: Sub sandwiches.

It's Burger Time
1620 First Avenue N., Moorhead, MN 56560
218-233-9641•www.itsburgertime.com

What you'll find: Burgers.

John Alexander's Restaurant
315 Main Avenue, Moorhead, MN 56560
218-287-5802

What you'll find: American food.

Sarello's Restaurant
28 Center Mall Avenue, Moorhead, MN 56560
218-287-0238•www.sarellos.com

What you'll find: American food.

Speak Easy Italian Restaurant
1001 Thirtieth Avenue S., Moorhead, MN 56560
218-233-1326•www.speakeasyrestaurant.com

What you'll find: Italian food.

Usher's House
700 First Avenue N., Moorhead, MN 56560
218-287-0080 • www.ushershouse.com

What you'll find: American food.

DETROIT LAKES

Chinese Dragon
808 Washington Avenue, Detroit Lakes, MN 56501
218-847-2177

What you'll find: Chinese food.

Fireside Restaurant
1462 E. Shore Drive, Detroit Lakes, MN 56501
218-847-8192 • www.firesidedl.com

What you'll find: American food.

It's Burger Time
214 Holmes Street E., Detroit Lakes, MN 56501
218-847-2974 • www.itsburgertime.com

What you'll find: Burgers.

Lakeside Tavern
200 W. Lake Drive, Detroit Lakes, MN 56501
218-847-1891 • www.lakesidetavern.com

What you'll find: American food.

Zorbaz on the Lake
402 W. Lake Drive, Detroit Lakes, MN 56501
218-847-5305•www.zorbaz.com

What you'll find: Pizza and Mexican food.

PARK RAPIDS

Beyond Juice
203 Main Avenue S., Park Rapids, MN 56470
218-732-0422

What you'll find: American food (soup, sandwiches, and smoothies).

The Good Life Café
220 Main Avenue S., Park Rapids, MN 56470
218-237-4212•www.thegoodlifecafepr.com

What you'll find: American food.

Great Northern Café
218 First Street E., Park Rapids, MN 56470
218-732-9565

What you'll find: American food.

Minnesoda Fountain
205 Main Avenue S., Park Rapids, MN 56470
218-732-3240

What you'll find: American food (soup and sandwiches).

Schwarzwald Restaurant
122 Main Avenue S., Park Rapids, MN 56470
218-732-8828

What you'll find: American and German food.

Zorbaz on the Lake
22036 County Road 7 N., Park Rapids, MN 56470
218-237-1969•www.zorbaz.com

What you'll find: Pizza and Mexican food.

WALKER

Boulders Restaurant
8363 Lake Land Trail NW, Walker, MN 56484
218-547-1006•thebouldersrestaurant.com

What you'll find: American food.

Café Zona Rosa
101 Fifth Street N., Walker, MN 56484
218-547-3558•www.cafezonarosa.com

What you'll find: Authentic Mexican food.

Charlie's Up North
6841 Minnesota Highway 371 NW, Walker, MN 56484
218-547-0222•www.charliesupnorth.com

What you'll find: American food.

Lucky Moose Bar & Grill
441 Walker Bay Boulevard, Walker, MN 56484
218-547-0801 • www.luckymoosebargrill.com

What you'll find: American food.

Ranch House Supper
9420 Minnesota Highway 371 NW, Walker, MN 56484
218-547-1540 • www.ranchhousesupperclub.com

What you'll find: American food.

Village Square Café
411 Minnesota Avenue W., Walker, MN 56484
218-547-1456 • www.villagesquarewalker.com

What you'll find: American food.

MOOSE LAKE

Art's Café
200 Arrowhead Lane, Moose Lake, MN 55767
218-485-4602

What you'll find: American food.

Joe Jitters Coffee House
308 Elm Avenue, Moose Lake, MN 55767
218-485-0660

What you'll find: Soup and sandwiches.

Lazy Moose Grille and Coffee House
300 S. Arrowhead Lane, Moose Lake, MN 55767
218-485-8712

What you'll find: American food.

Poor Gary's Pizza
401 Elm Avenue, Moose Lake, MN 55767
218-485-8020

What you'll find: Pizza and sub sandwiches.

BARNUM

Lazy Bear Grill
3696 Main Street, Barnum, MN 55707
218-389-6991

What you'll find: American food (pizza and burgers).

Lou's Rustic Diner
3729 Front Street, Barnum, MN 55707
218-389-6084 • www.lousrusticdiner.com

What you'll find: American food.

SANDSTONE

Jan & Gary's Country Dining
945 Minnesota Highway 23 N., Sandstone, MN 55072
320-245-0109

What you'll find: American food (family style).

Kitty's Corner Café
421 Commercial Avenue N., Sandstone, MN 55072
320-245-3114

What you'll find: American food.

HINCKLEY

Cassidy's Restaurant
327 Fire Monument Road, Hinckley, MN 55037
320-384-6129

What you'll find: American food.

Final Score
104 Main Street E., Hinckley, MN 55037
320-384-7855

What you'll find: American food and homemade pizza.

Fire Storm Café
119 Main Street E., Hinckley, MN 55037
320-384-0505

What you'll find: American food and pizza.

Rosie's Place Café
304 Old Highway 61 S., Hinckley, MN 55037
320-384-6209

What you'll find: American food.

Tobies Restaurant & Bakery
404 Fire Monument Road, Hinckley, MN 55037
320-384-6174 • www.tobies.com

What you'll find: American food.

PINE CITY

Cabin Coffee's
805 Sixth Street SW, Pine City, MN 55063
320-629-5982 • www.cabincoffees.com

What you'll find: Coffees and American food.

New China
150 Main Street S., Pine City, MN 55063
320-629-6365

What you'll find: Chinese food.

Nicolls Café
255 Main Street S., Pine City, MN 55063
320-629-6833

What you'll find: American food.

BRECKENRIDGE

Good Luck Chinese Restaurant
230 Minnesota Avenue, Breckenridge, MN 56520
218-643-8212

What you'll find: Chinese food.

Northern Grille
739 US Highway 75, Breckenridge, MN 56520
218-643-5301

What you'll find: American food.

Wilkin Drink & Eatery
508 Minnesota Avenue, Breckenridge, MN 56520
218-643-3862

What you'll find: American food.

Bed and
Breakfast

Wildwood Inn Bed & Breakfast
3361 Cottonwood Road NW, Baudette, MN 56623
218-634-1356 or 888-212-7031 • www.wildwoodinnbb.com

Amenities: Five guest bedroom suites, each with a private bathroom. Common area with large-screen TV and satellite TV service, and wireless Internet access. Gourmet meals, Sunday buffets, private dinners, picnic lunches, and dining for special diets can be arranged. The 100-acre property is at the mouth of the Rainy River on Lake of the Woods.

Features you'll appreciate: Dining room has coffee and beverage service and snacks; guests have access to the commercial kitchen, and no charge for long distance calls.

Directions: Take Minnesota Highway 172 north twelve miles to Lake of the Woods and turn left onto Cottonwood Road, a circle drive. Turn into the second Cottonwood Road across from Border Bait Co. into the driveway straight ahead.

Hundred Acre Woods Bed & Breakfast
5048 Old Highway 53, Orr, MN 55771
218-757-0070 • www.voyageurcountry.com/HundredAcreWoods

Amenities: Two guest rooms. Log Cabin Room: cedar log queen-sized bed, private sauna, and bath. Master Bear Room: spindle headboard queen-sized bed, double Jacuzzi in room, and private bathroom.

Features you'll appreciate: Snowmobile rentals, snowshoes included with stay, massage available by appointment, fire pit, fireplace, DSL available, satellite TV, and a swing on the deck.

Directions: From US Highway 53 at Orr, go three-and-a-half miles north, take a right on Old Highway 53, and go a half-mile.

Willow Creek Bed and Breakfast
14242 430th Street SE, Fertile, MN 56540
218-945-6315 • www.willowcreek-fertile.com

Amenities: Three guest rooms with 1940s décor in restored 1918 home. All rooms have air conditioning, satellite TV with DVD, clock radio/CD player, and in-room coffee, tea, or cocoa.

Features you'll appreciate: Includes a farm breakfast served every morning at 8 a.m. in the dining room.

Directions: From Fertile, take County Road 1 five miles east, turn north at large sign (140th Avenue SE) and drive one mile; take right (east) at 430th Street SE and go about eight miles to the B&B.

Villa Calma Bed & Breakfast
915 Lake Blvd NE, Bemidji, MN 56601
218-444-5554 • www.villacalma.com

Amenities: Four guest rooms in restored 1910 house with pillowtop mattresses, down pillows, warm blankets, goose down duvets and duvet covers, Egyptian cotton bath sheets, and robes. Rooms with antiques and new furnishings, and air conditioning.

Features you'll appreciate: Free wireless high-speed Internet access and view of Lake Bemidji.

Directions: In Bemidji, follow Minnesota Highway 197 (Paul Bunyan Drive) north to Sixth Street. Turn right and follow the street curving to the left (turns into Lake Boulevard). Continue to Tenth Street and turn left, then take the next left onto Dewey Avenue.

My Lake Home Bed & Breakfast
50917 E. Dixon Lake Road, Squaw Lake, MN 56681
218-659-4797 • www.mylakeome.com

Amenities: Two guest rooms with toiletries, robes, complimentary slippers, and bath and beach towels provided. Happy hour, snacks, and four-course breakfast.

Features you'll appreciate: Wireless Internet; free guest kitchenette and gas grill; coffee, tea, and popcorn upon request; laundry center and soaps; campfire wood and S'mores; paddleboats, canoes, kayaks, floaters, and dock space; fax and telephone; TV-free zone, and billiards and game table; groomed cross-country ski trails.

Directions: From Grand Rapids, take US Highway 2 west through Deer River, turn right on Minnesota Highway 46 (twenty-nine miles) to County Road 32, left (five miles) to County Road 156, left (three miles) to E. Dixon Lake Road, right (half a mile) to Milakome Drive.

Morning Glory Bed & Breakfast
726 NW Second Avenue, Grand Rapids, MN 55744
218-326-3978 or 866-926-3978 • www.morningglorybandb.com

Amenities: Four two-room suites with sitting room and private baths, three with fireplaces and one with a whirlpool. TV, cable, phone, and air conditioning. Full breakfast with flexible times. Water, tea, hot chocolate, and cookies are always available. Wine and hors d'oeuvres served on weekends.

Features you'll appreciate: Living room offers a wood-burning fireplace, piano, library, and game area with terrace door to a private guest patio.

Directions: From US highways 169 and 2 in Grand Rapids, follow Highway 2 west to Minnesota Highway 38, go north three blocks to Eighth Street E. one block to Second Avenue NW and south a half-block.

Northern Comfort Bed & Breakfast

4776 Waisanen Road, Embarrass, MN 55732
218-984-2014 • www.northerncomfortmn.com

Amenities: Five bedrooms with down comforters in a 1910 former Finnish boarding house; traditional Finnish sauna; wireless Internet; refrigerator; snacks: popcorn, gourmet coffee, hot tea, cocoa, fruit juice, and filtered water. Snow shoes and cross-country skis available. Flexible check-in and check-out times.

Features you'll appreciate: Wine, cheese and crackers, and dessert served in the evenings. Country breakfast served in the morning.

Directions: From County Highway 21 at Embarrass, go one-half mile south on County Road 362 (Waisnanen Road).

Blue Heron Bed & Breakfast

827 Kawishiwi Trail, Ely, MN 55731
218-365-4720 • www.blueheronbnb.com

Amenities: Five lake-view rooms, king- and queen-sized beds, private bath, sauna, rocking chairs, and fine dining overlooking the lake. Trails nearby for hiking, biking, and skiing. Canoes, kayaks, and snowshoes available.

Features you'll appreciate: Lakeside lodge located on the border of the Boundary Waters Canoe Area Wilderness. Special dietary needs accommodated.

Directions: From Ely, go north on US Highway 169 two miles to Kawishiwi Trail (County Road 58, which turns into County Road 16), then turn right and go two miles to Silver Rapids Bridge. After four miles the road will go back to gravel, continue one-tenth mile to driveway on left marked with sign.

MacArthur House Bed & Breakfast
520 W. Second Street, Grand Marais, MN 55604
218-387-1840 or 800-792-1840•www.macarthurhouse.net

Amenities: Six guestrooms all have private bathrooms, with showers or tubs. Free Wi-Fi.
Features you'll appreciate: Open year-round.
Directions: From Minnesota Highway 61 coming into Grand Marais, turn left at Sixth Avenue, drive up the hill two blocks to the corner of W. Second Street.

Pincushion Bed & Breakfast
968 Gunflint Trail, Grand Marais, MN 55604
218-387-2969•www.pincushionbb.com

Amenities: Four wood-paneled guest rooms with private baths and showers. Most rooms have views of sunrises over Lake Superior, and the common area has a fireplace and attached deck. Breakfast may be a warm fruit compote, wild rice vegetable frittata, and homemade muffins, or chilled fruit soup, baked apple pancake, and turkey sausage.
Features you'll appreciate: Good for hikers, canoeists, bikers, cross-country skiers, and snowshoers. Boundary Waters Canoe Area Wilderness entry points are thirty minutes away. In winter, ski out the front door onto the twenty-five kilometer Pincushion Trail system.
Directions: Three miles north of Grand Marais on Gunflint Trail (County Road 12) near the top of the hill; look for Pincushion B&B sign and turn right.

Baptism River Inn Bed and Breakfast
6125 Minnesota Highway 1, Silver Bay, MN 55614
877-353-0707 or 218-353-0707•www.baptismriverinn.com

Amenities: Four guest rooms with reading chairs, and private baths with whirlpool tubs. The Suite, River and Sunset rooms all have balconies. The Suite has a full-size sleeper.
Features you'll appreciate: Trails and parks within minutes of the bed and breakfast for hiking, skiing, snowshoeing, and more.
Directions: From Minnesota Highway 61 at Illgen City, turn inland on Highway 1 and go three miles.

Lighthouse Bed & Breakfast
1 LightHouse Point, Two Harbors, MN 55616
888-832-5606•http://lighthousebb.org

Amenities: Four guest rooms, each with a view of Lake Superior, common bathroom, breakfast in the common rooms.
Features you'll appreciate: The Skiff House has a private bathroom with a Jacuzzi tub (no shower).
Directions: From the north end of Two Harbors on Minnesota Highway 61, turn toward Lake Superior onto First Street and go to South Avenue, turn right. Continue two blocks to Third Street and turn left, go two blocks.

Solglimt Bed & Breakfast
828 Lake Avenue S., Duluth, MN 55802
218-727-0596 or 877-727-0596•www.solglimt.com

Amenities: Five suites with private baths, fireplaces, and contemporary furnishings. Recognized for "green" efforts. All rooms have good views.
Features you'll appreciate: Beach, steps away from Lake Superior and one block past Duluth's Canal Park.

Directions: From Interstate 35, take Exit 256B (Fifth Avenue W./Lake Avenue) and follow signs to Canal Park and Park Point, cross the Aerial Lift Bridge and go to the twelfth house on the left.

A.G. Thomson House Bed & Breakfast
2617 E. Third Street, Duluth, MN 55812
218-724-3464 or 877-807-8077 • http://thomsonhouse.biz

Amenities: Seven rooms with private baths, six with oversized whirlpools and Jacuzzi tubs; views of Lake Superior; fireplace; flat-screen TV and DVD, and iPod docking station; wine and drinking glasses; four rooms offer a refrigerator.

Features you'll appreciate: Free high-speed wireless Internet access and a DVD library with more than 500 movies.

Directions: From Interstate 35 in Duluth, go inland at S. Twenty-Sixth Avenue E. and turn right at E. Third Street.

Olcott House Bed and Breakfast Inn
2316 E. First Street, Duluth, MN 55812
218-728-1339 or 800-715-1339 • www.olcotthouse.com

Amenities: Six private suites in mansion with fireplaces, private baths, satellite TV, and DVD library. Full candlelight breakfast, plus afternoon wine and cheese. Views of the harbor.

Features you'll appreciate: Library and music room with grand piano.

Directions: Take Interstate 35 north past downtown Duluth to Exit 258 (E. Twenty-First Avenue) and drive uphill four blocks to E. Superior Street, turn right. Take second left on N. Twenty-Third Avenue E. and go one block to E. First Street and turn right.

Cotton Mansion Bed & Breakfast
2309 E. First Street, Duluth, MN 55812
218-724-6405 or 800-228-1997 • www.cottonmansion.com

Amenities: Seven guest rooms in mansion with two-person whirlpools, fireplaces, private baths, and a gourmet breakfast.
Features you'll appreciate: Close to Duluth attractions such as Canal Park and the Aerial Lift Bridge, and local dining and shopping.
Directions: Take Interstate 35 north past downtown Duluth to Exit 258 (E. Twenty-First Avenue) and drive uphill four blocks to E. Superior Street, turn right. Take second left on N. Twenty-Third Avenue E. and go one block to E. First Street and turn right.

The Ellery House Bed & Breakfast
28 S. Twenty-First Avenue E., Duluth, MN 55812
218-724-7639 or 800-355-3794 • www.elleryhouse.com

Amenities: Four guest rooms in Victorian inn include breakfasts that can be served in the room, fireplaces, private baths, deep clawfoot soaking tubs, antiques, air conditioning, and refrigerators.
Features you'll appreciate: Anniversary and romance packages; near the Rose Gardens overlooking Lake Superior.
Directions: Take Interstate 35 north past downtown Duluth to Exit 258 (E. Twenty-First Avenue) and go uphill for two blocks. Turn right at the first driveway above Jefferson Street.

Heritage Rose Bed and Breakfast
104 Front Street E., Hitterdal, MN 56552
218-962-3425

Amenities: Two guest rooms with queen-sized beds and private bathrooms, with fireplace in one of the rooms; complimentary breakfast; open in fall and winter.

Features you'll appreciate: Across from the city park.

Directions: From US Highway 10 between Moorhead and Detroit Lakes, go north seven miles on Minnesota Highway 32 to Hitterdal and right on Front Street.

Mulberry Row Bed & Breakfast on Little Pelican Lake
25856 Dahl Road, Detroit Lakes, MN 56501
218-532-2263 • www.mulberryrow.com

Amenities: Three guest rooms with queen-sized beds. Includes a fireplace room as well as a media room with a large-screen TV with Surround Sound, satellite service, and DVD movies, a computer room with Internet access, and leather furniture with six reclining seats.

Features you'll appreciate: The dining room offers hot coffee and fresh baked foods in the morning.

Directions: From Detroit Lakes, take US Highway 59 south to County Road 20, turn west and go two miles to Pinewood Road, turn left and drive toward the lake, and turn right on Dahl Road.

LoonSong Bed & Breakfast
17248 Loonsong Lane, Park Rapids, MN 56470
218-266-3333 or 888-825-8135 • www.loonsongbedandbreakfast.com

Amenities: Four guest rooms; queen-sized beds; private bath with double vanity, shower and tub; refrigerator; and private patio. Furnished with antiques and collectibles.

Features you'll appreciate: A basket with coffee and muffins delivered to your door around 7:30 a.m., with breakfast served until 8:30 or 9:00. The menu can include peach panakokens and homemade sausages; raspberry French toast with whipped cream and raspberries on top; or eggs, bacon, caramel sweet rolls, pancakes with blueberries, fresh fruit, and coffee.

Directions: From Park Rapids, go north on US Highway 71 to Highway 200 west (left), past east and north entrance of Itasca State Park, and watch for mile marker 83; turn left on Anchor Matson Road and follow the LoonSong signs for three miles.

Heartland Trail Bed & Breakfast
20220 Friar Road, Park Rapids, MN 56470
218-732-3252 • www.heartlandbb.com

Amenities: Each room in this former schoolhouse has a twelve-foot ceiling, an in-room bathroom, a gas fireplace, and a TV. Select rooms have a DVD player, compact refrigerator, and microwave.

Features you'll appreciate: Full breakfast is served. The B&B is near the Heartland State Trail bike path and offers on-site bike rental. Child friendly.

Directions: From Park Rapids, take Minnesota Highway 34 east about five miles to Minnesota Highway 226. Turn north and go one mile into the village of Dorset.

The Park Street Inn
106 Park Street, Nevis, MN 56467
218-652-4500 • www.parkstreetinn.com

Amenities: Across from public beach overlooking Lake Belle Taine and a block from the Heartland State Trail. Four rooms with private baths and air conditioning. The Suite includes an all-season porch and double whirlpool. The Grotto room includes an oversize whirlpool and a waterfall sink.

Features you'll appreciate: Full breakfast is served. Bridal suites are available. Open year-round.

Directions: From Minnesota Highway 34 at Nevis, turn north at County Highway 2 (Main Street), go one block and turn left onto Park Street and go half a block.

Embracing Pines Bed & Breakfast
32287 Mississippi Road, Walker, MN 56484
218-224-3519 or 218-731-5026 • www.embracingpines.com

Amenities: Three guest rooms, breakfasts, birdwatching, and shuttle service that covers both the Heartland and Paul Bunyan trails.
Features you'll appreciate: Located on the Paul Bunyan State Trail.
Directions: From Walker, go four miles west on Minnesota 371/200 and turn left on Highway 200 toward Laporte and Benedict. Go two and one-half miles to County Road 38 at Benedict. Turn left onto County Road 38, and left again on Mississippi Road.

Home in the Pines Bed & Breakfast Inn
88816 Wild Oak Loop, Duquette, MN 55756
218-496-5825 or 218-496-5855 • www.homeinthepinesbb.com

Amenities: Two guest rooms on the second floor; common area outside the guest rooms has refrigerator, coffeemaker, TV, games, and books; front porch has rockers, tables, and chairs.
Features you'll appreciate: Country breakfast is served in the dining room on the first floor each morning.
Directions: Take Interstate 35 north from Minneapolis-St. Paul to Exit 195 (Finlayson/Askov) and turn right onto Minnesota Highway 23. Go twenty-five miles to Duquette and turn left on County Road 47 just past the Duquette General Store. Go a quarter-mile and turn right onto Wild Oak Loop; take the left fork in the driveway.

Giese Bed and Breakfast Inn

13398 130th Avenue, Finlayson, MN 55735

320-233-6429 or 888-220-0234 • www.giese-bnb.com

Amenities: Four guest rooms in newly constructed inn, each with private baths, queen-sized bed, comforters, and extra pillows. Each room has its own thermostat, an air conditioner, and a French door to an outer deck.

Features you'll appreciate: Books, games, puzzles, and a TV by a fireplace in the lounge. Antiques/collectibles store on premises.

Directions: From Interstate 35, take Exit 195 to Banning Junction. Take Minnesota Highway 18 west through Finlayson and go ten miles. Turn left in Giese onto County Road 23 and go south half a mile.

Woodland Trails Bed & Breakfast

40361 Grace Lake Road, Hinckley, MN 55037

320-655-3901 • http://woodlandtrails.net

Amenities: Five guest rooms, each with an electric fireplace, comfortable chairs for reading or lounging, and a private deck. Second-floor rooms have a queen-sized bed, and private baths with shower and whirlpool tub. Three-course breakfast is included; guest refrigerator offers complimentary snacks and beverages.

Features you'll appreciate: Take a paddle boat or canoe on Grace Lake Too, visit a pond stocked with bass and bluegills, or hike on one of the private trails.

Directions: From Interstate 35 at Hinckley, take Minnesota Highway 48 east for twenty-three miles to the St. Croix River, turn left (north) on Grace Lake Road and go half a mile.

Campgrounds

Lake Bronson State Park Campground

3793 230th Street (County Road 28), Lake Bronson, MN 56734
218-754-2200
www.dnr.state.mn.us/state_parks/lake_bronson/camping.html

Amenities: 152 drive-in campsites, sixty-seven with electricity, and biking and hiking trails during the spring, summer, and fall seasons. Three hike-in campsites and two canoe-in campsites.
Features you'll appreciate: Six pull-through campsites. Wi-Fi on lakeside campgrounds.
Directions: Two miles east of the town of Lake Bronson with park access on County Highway 28.

Bemis Hill Campground

Thompson Forest Road, Wannaska, MN 56761
218-425-7504

Amenities: Two primitive campsites, four primitive horse campsites, cleared area, fire ring, table, vault toilets, garbage cans, and drinking water.
Features you'll appreciate: Winter sledding slope, a shelter, and access to snowmobile trails, hunting, and berry picking near the campground.
Directions: From Wannaska, take Minnesota Highway 89 one mile to County Road 4; turn left and go 8.6 miles, take Thompson Forest Road 6.2 miles to Bemis Hill.

Hayes Lake State Park Campground
48990 County Road 4, Roseau, MN 56751
218-425-7504
www.dnr.state.mn.us/state_parks/hayes_lake/camping.html

Amenities: Thirty-five drive-in sites, eighteen with electric hookups; campground is open in the fall; on-site swimming beach and fishing boat motors. Thirteen miles of hiking, five miles of mountain biking, eleven miles of cross-country skiing, and six miles of snowmobile trails.
Features you'll appreciate: Two rustic camper cabins; they can accommodate five to six people and include electricity.
Directions: Fifteen miles south of Roseau on Minnesota Highway 89, then nine miles east on County Road 4.

Zippel Bay State Park Campground
3684 Fifty-Fourth Avenue NW, Williams, MN 56686
218-783-6252
www.dnr.state.mn.us/state_parks/zippel_bay/camping.html

Amenities: Fifty-seven drive-in sites, accessible to the disabled, flush toilets, group camp facilities, hot showers, pets allowed, sanitary dump station, secluded campsites, and a swimming beach.
Features you'll appreciate: Open in the fall and winter.
Directions: From the west end of Baudette, take Minnesota Highway 172 ten miles north to County Road 8. Go west for six miles to park entrance.

Ash River Campground
County Road 126, Orr, MN 55771
218-365-7229
www.dnr.state.mn.us/state_forests/facilities/cmp00029/index.html

Amenities: Eight primitive campsites in the Kabetogama State Forest, two picnic tables, swimming, fishing, cleared area, fire ring, table, vault toilets, garbage cans, and drinking water.
Features you'll appreciate: Hiking, water access including boat ramp, whitewater paddling on the Ash River, and access to Voyageurs National Park.
Directions: From Orr, take US Highway 53 north twenty-six miles to Ash River Road (County Road 126); turn right (east) and go ten miles.

Union Lake Sarah Campground
20049 Campground Road SE, Erskine, MN 56535
218-687-5155 or 218-687-3969

Amenities: Seventy-one campsites (five are tent-only), electricity, water, pets allowed in campsites, accessible to disabled, flush toilets, hot showers, hiking trail, and secluded campsites.
Features you'll appreciate: A swimming beach, fishing boats, canoes and kayaks, lake and river access (boat ramp), dock space, slips and mooring buoys, pontoon boats, and a playground.
Directions: From the junction of US highways 2 and 59, take Highway 59 south two miles, go west on County Road H for approximately four miles, then left.

Fox Lake Campground
2556 Island View Drive NE, Bemidji, MN 56601
218-586-2231 • www.camponfoxlake.com

Amenities: Lakeside, lake view, and pull-through sites for all types of campers. Seventy sites with 20/30/50 amp electrical, water, and sewer. Cable TV and telephone. Some sites are close to accessible restrooms and laundry facilities.

Features you'll appreciate: Wi-Fi, cable TV, game room, playground, volleyball and basketball courts, boat ramps and docks, restroom, and shower with laundry facilities, and deck overlooking the lake.

Directions: From Bemidji go north on US Highway 71 3.6 miles to the County Road 15 (Irvine Avenue) off-ramp. Take a left and go north on County Road 15 3.75 miles to County Road 22 E. (Island View Drive NE). Then right for 3.3 miles.

Mosomo Point Campground
1037 Division Street, Deer River, MN 56636
218-246-2123 • www.us-parks.com/camping/mn/
mosomo-point-campground.html

Amenities: Boating, jet skiing, water skiing, boat ramp and dock, canoeing, swimming, fishing, fish cleaning station, fire rings, firewood, garbage service, gas and propane, grills, hiking trail, hunting, interpretive programs, mountain biking, picnic tables, recycling, tent pads, flush toilets, and vault toilets.

Features you'll appreciate: Berry picking, bicycle riding, bike trails, nature trails, sightseeing, wildlife viewing, and birdwatching.

Directions: Nineteen miles north of Deer River on Minnesota Highway 46. Turn west on Forest Road 2190 a half-mile past the Cut Foot Sioux Information Center.

Clubhouse Lake Campground
Marcell, MN 56657
218-246-2123

Amenities: Forty-seven sites, sandy swim beach, accessible fishing pier, biking, boat launch, fire rings, firewood, hiking trails, restrooms, and day-use area.

Features you'll appreciate: Water access to several lakes is possible with smaller boats or canoes. The Rice River canoe route starts at the Bigfork River from waters that flow into Clubhouse Lake.
Directions: From Minnesota Highway 38 in Marcell, go five miles east on County Road 45, then three miles north on Forest Road 2181 to the entrance.

Owen Lake State Forest Campground
County Road 52, Bigfork, MN 56628
218-743-3362
www.dnr.state.mn.us/state_forests/facilities/cmp00024/index.html

Amenities: Primitive campsites in the George Washington State Forest consist of a cleared area, fire ring, and table. Twenty campsites along lakeshore.
Features you'll appreciate: Vault toilets, one Dumpster, and drinking water. Open in the fall and pets are allowed.
Directions: From Bigfork, Minnesota, take Scenic Highway (County Road 7) southeast ten miles to County Road 340; go left (east) approximately seven miles to County Road 52; turn left (northeast) and follow signs two miles.

McCarthy Beach State Park Campground
7622 McCarthy Beach Road, Side Lake, MN 55781
218-254-7979
www.dnr.state.mn.us/state_parks/mccarthy_beach/camping.html

Amenities: Eighty-six drive-in sites, eighteen with electric hookups, plus three walk-in sites and group camp; accessible to disabled, flush toilets, hot showers; daily site rentals, swimming beach, bike trail, cross-country ski trail, hiking trail, and snowmobile trail; canoes, kayaks, fishing boats, and lake and river access.

Features you'll appreciate: Open in the winter and fall, and pets allowed. Access to state horse and snowmobile trails.
Directions: From Hibbing, take US Highway 169 north to County Road 5, then follow that north fifteen miles to the park.

Fenske Lake Campground
2229 Echo Trail, Ely, MN 55731
218-235-1299

Amenities: Fourteen shaded campsites with picnic table, fire grate, and tent pad; solar-electric pump for drinking water; biking, boat ramp, canoe rental, fishing, nature trails, swimming, and wildlife viewing. Near access points to the Boundary Waters Canoe Area Wilderness; the lake is part of a Superior National Forest canoe circle route.
Features you'll appreciate: An open log shelter is near the picnic area.
Directions: From Ely, go east on US Highway 169 north (toward Winton) for about one mile; turn left onto County Road 88 and go about two miles. Turn right onto the Echo Trail and continue about seven miles to the entrance on the right.

Birch Lake Campground
11580 Little Lake Road, Ely, MN 55731
218-235-1299

Amenities: Twenty-nine campsites, five tent-only sites, one group camp located near Big Birch Lake, accessible to disabled, daily site rentals, swimming beach, bike trail, hiking trail, snowmobile trail, boat landing, canoe rental, vault toilets, and a hand pump for drinking water. Near the Boundary Waters Canoe Area Wilderness in the Superior National Forest; motorboats are allowed on the lake. Birdwatching, photography, and interpretive programs offered.

Features you'll appreciate: Open in the fall, and pets allowed.

Directions: From Ely, go south on Minnesota Highway 1 for about eight miles, until Forest Road 429 (Little Lake Road). Turn right and continue for four miles to the entrance; turn left and continue one mile to the campground.

Bear Head Lake State Park Campground
9301 Bear Head State Park Road, Ely, MN 55731
218-365-7229
www.dnr.state.mn.us/state_parks/bear_head_lake/index.html

Amenities: Seventy-three campsites (forty-five electric), three campsites for winter camping, RV length limit sixty feet, four backpack sites, two canoe sites, camper cabins, and one group site that accommodates up to fifty people.

Features you'll appreciate: Hiking trails, swimming beach, lake and river access for boats, dock space, slips and mooring buoys, and fishing boats, canoes, kayaks, and fishing boat motors are available. Snowshoes, groomed cross-country ski trail and snowmobile trail.

Directions: From Tower, take US Highway 169 east nine miles to County Highway 128, then go south seven miles to the park.

Twin Lakes Campsites
Lima Mountain Road, Grand Marais, MN 55604
218-387-3039
www.dnr.state.mn.us/state_forests/facilities/cmp00067/index.html

Amenities: Three primitive campsites in the Pat Bayle State Forest, fishing, cleared area, fire ring, table, and garbage cans.

Features you'll appreciate: All sites are on a first-come, first-served basis.

Directions: From Minnesota Highway 61 in Grand Marais, take Gunflint Trail to S. Brule Road; turn left (west) six miles to Lima Mountain Road and then left (south) four miles.

Little Isabella River Campground
Tofte MN 55615
218-663-7280

Amenities: Eleven nonelectric sites, pit restrooms, firewood, fishing, flush toilets, grills, hiking, and picnic tables.
Features you'll appreciate: Birdwatching and wildlife viewing.
Directions: From Minnesota Highway 61 at Illgen City, turn inland on Minnesota Highway 1 and follow it to Isabella. Continue 4.5 miles west of Isabella to the entrance.

Temperance River State Park Campground
7620 W. Minnesota Highway 61, Schroeder, MN 55613
218-663-7476
www.dnr.state.mn.us/state_parks/temperance_river/camping.html

Amenities: Two campgrounds, an upper and a lower, with fifty-two campsites—eighteen with 30-amp electrical hookups and six cart-in sites; most sites are well spaced in a shaded, wooded area; flush toilets and showers available mid-May through September. Shower building is located in the upper campground.
Features you'll appreciate: Hiking and snowmobile trails, self-guided nature trails, waterfalls, and spruce, cedar, and birch forests. Ten electric campsites in the upper campground are available year-round.
Directions: Entrance is one mile north of Schroeder on Highway 61.

Tettegouche State Park Campground
5702 Minnesota Highway 61, Silver Bay, MN 55614
218-226-6365
www.dnr.state.mn.us/state_parks/tettegouche/camping.html

Amenities: Twenty-eight drive-in campsites (twenty-two with electric hookups), five backpack sites, six walk-in sites, thirteen cart-in sites, five kayak sites, and two group camps. Accessible to disabled, flush toilets, group camp facilities, hot showers, lodge and central building, daily site rentals, bike trail, cross-country ski trail, hiking trail, and snowmobile trail.

Features you'll appreciate: On the North Shore of Lake Superior, open in the fall and winter, and pets allowed.

Directions: Entrance to the park is four-and-a-half miles northeast of Silver Bay on Highway 61.

Finland State Forest Campground
County Road 6, Finland, MN 55603
218-226-6365
www.dnr.state.mn.us/state_forests/facilities/cmp00016/index.html

Amenities: Thirty-nine primitive campsites, boat launch, cleared area, fire ring, and picnic table, vault toilets, garbage cans, and drinking water.

Features you'll appreciate: Campsites are located about seven miles from Lake Superior and Tettegouche State Park at the Baptism River. Access to ATV trails.

Directions: From Minnesota Highway 61 at Illgen City, turn inland on Minnesota Highway 1 to Finland, then take County Road 6 about a half-mile to the campground.

Eckbeck State Forest Campground
Minnesota Highway 1, Silver Bay, MN 55614
218-226-6365
www.dnr.state.mn.us/state_forests/facilities/cmp00015/index.html

Amenities: Thirty-one campsites, cleared area, fire ring, picnic table, vault toilets, garbage cans, and drinking water.

Features you'll appreciate: Three miles from Lake Superior and Tettegouche State Park, adjacent to the Baptism River.

Directions: From Minnesota Highway 61 at Illgen City, turn inland on Highway 1 and go three-and-a-half miles to the campground.

Split Rock Lighthouse State Park Campground
3755 Split Rock Lighthouse Road, Two Harbors, MN 55616
218-226-6377
www.dnr.state.mn.us/state_parks/Split_rock_lighthouse/camping.html

Amenities: Twenty-four tent-only campsites, ten available in the winter (twenty are cart-in, four are backpack sites); twelve miles of hiking trail, eight miles of paved bike trail, cross-country skiing, and snowshoeing; lake, river, and stream fishing; flush toilets and hot showers; pets allowed in campsite; open fall and winter; accessible to disabled.

Features you'll appreciate: Split Rock Lighthouse historic site is located in the park with tours and visitor center.

Directions: Twenty miles northeast of Two Harbors on Minnesota Highway 61.

Cadotte Lake Campground
318 Forestry Road, Aurora, MN 55705
218-229-8819

Amenities: Twenty-seven campsites, RVs up to forty-five feet long, fishing platform, boat landing and dock, picnic area, hand pump, and restrooms.

Features you'll appreciate: Playground area and sandy beach.

Directions: From Two Harbors, take County Highway 2 north for twenty-five miles; turn west on County Road 15 and travel twelve miles. Turn north and go six-tenths of a mile on Forest Road 425, then turn and go southwest on Forest Road 778 for one mile to the campground.

Indian Lake State Forest Campground
Off County Road 44, Two Harbors, MN 55616
218-226-6377
www.dnr.state.mn.us/state_forests/facilities/cmp00009/index.html

Amenities: Twenty-five primitive drive-in campsites and one group campsite, cleared area, fire ring, table, vault toilets, garbage cans, and drinking water. Swimming, water access including boat ramp, and access to hiking trails.

Features you'll appreciate: Canoe access to the Cloquet River State Water Trail.

Directions: From Minnesota Highway 61 at Two Harbors, take County Road 2 north thirteen miles; turn left onto County Road 14 and continue for ten miles; turn right onto County Road 44 and continue for 1.2 miles; turn left at the entrance.

Sullivan Lake State Forest Campground
Off County Road 15 (Forest Highway 11), Two Harbors, MN 55616
218-226-6377
www.dnr.state.mn.us/state_forests/facilities/cmp00017/index.html

Amenities: Eleven primitive campsites, cleared area, fire ring, table, vault toilets, garbage cans, drinking water, boat launch, nature trails, and four day-use picnic sites.

Features you'll appreciate: All sites are on a first-come, first-served basis for a fee. Access to Sullivan Lake.

Directions: From Minnesota Highway 61 in Two Harbors, take County Road 2 north twenty-six miles to County Road 15; turn left (west) and go a half-mile; turn left (south) at Sullivan Lake Road entrance.

Spirit Mountain Campground
9500 Spirit Mountain Place, Duluth, MN 55810
218-628-2891, 218-624-8544, or 800-642-6377, ext. 544
www.spiritmt.com/camping/

Amenities: Seventy-three campsites, thirty-nine with water hookups, walk-in tenting, fire pits, picnic tables and electricity, and two shower buildings.

Features you'll appreciate: Access to water, hiking, and biking trails — a trailhead for the Superior Hiking Trail is within walking distance. Convenient to Duluth attractions.

Directions: From Interstate 35, take Exit 249 and follow the frontage road signs to campground office on the right side of the road.

Itasca State Park Campgrounds
36750 Main Park Drive, Park Rapids, MN 56470
218-699-7251 • www.dnr.state.mn.us/state_parks/itasca/camping.html

Amenities: The park has 223 drive-in sites in two campgrounds, with 160 electric sites; RV length limit is sixty feet; four sites are handicapped accessible; eleven backpack sites and eleven sites offer carts to haul gear; showers, accessible flush toilets, and vault toilets.

Features you'll appreciate: Group camp accommodates up to fifty people.

Directions: South entrance to the park is twenty-three miles north of Park Rapids on US Highway 71. From Bemidji, the east entrance is thirty miles south on Highway 71 and one-tenth mile north on Minnesota Highway 200. The north entrance is twenty miles south of Bagley on Minnesota highways 92 and 200.

Akeley City Campground and Park
355 Crow Wing Lake Drive NE, Akeley, MN 56433
218-252-4570•www.akeleyminnesota.com/park_camp/park.htm

Amenities: Twenty-four lakeside campsites on 11th Crow Wing Lake, including electric and water hookups and grassy tent area; public boat access, fishing pier, fish cleaning house, fire rings, dump station, picnic shelter, showers, flush restrooms, sandy swimming beach, and playground.

Features you'll appreciate: Camping season starts the second weekend in May and goes through September. Access to the Heartland State Trail.

Directions: From intersection of Minnesota highways 64 and 34 in Akeley, go one block east and turn left (north) on County Highway 23 (Pleasant Avenue NE), then go left on Crow Wing Lake Drive NE.

Baker and White Oak Lake Campsites
Land O'Lakes State Forest, Remer, MN 56672
218-833-8710• www.dnr.state.mn.us/state_forests/facilities/
cmp00069/index.html

Amenities: Two primitive campsites, cleared area, fire ring, and table.

Features you'll appreciate: Campsites are adjacent to the Moose River ATV Trail. All sites are on a first-come, first-served basis.

Directions: From Outing, take Minnesota Highway 6 north seven miles to Draper Tower Forest Road, then go right (east) 3.5 miles on forest road and ATV trail.

Shell City Horse Campground
Huntersville State Forest, Menahga, MN 56464
218-266-2100
www.dnr.state.mn.us/state_forests/facilities/cmp00027/index.html

Amenities: Twenty-seven horse sites, eight camp sites, vault toilets, drinking water, river access, swimming, and fishing.

Features you'll appreciate: On a twenty-four mile horse trail that includes two loops and a river crossing.

Directions: From Menahga, take Stocking Lake Road east four miles to County Road 23; turn left (north) one mile to 380th Street; turn right (east) three miles to 199th Avenue; turn left (north) one mile.

St. Croix Haven Campground
40756 Grace Lake Road, Hinckley, MN 55037
320-655-7989 or 800-280-0166 • www.stcroixhavencampground.com

Amenities: Three-season campground, cul-de-sac campsites, miles of trails in the hundred acres of forests, wildlife, scenic St. Croix River, inner tube float trips, canoeing, fishing, and indoor pool.

Features you'll appreciate: End-of-the-day campfire with roasting marshmallows, and favorite stories or songs.

Directions: From Interstate 35, take Exit 183 at Hinckley and go east on Minnesota Highway 48 for twenty-three miles. Just before the Minnesota/Wisconsin border, go left on County Road 173 (Grace Lake Road) and go one mile.

Hotels and Motels

Gateway Motel & Museum
702 S. Atlantic, Hallock, MN 56728
218-843-2032

Amenities: Three double rooms and six single rooms. All rooms include microwaves, refrigerators, cable television, free wireless Internet, and coffee maker. Pet friendly.
Features you'll appreciate: On-site museum display with toys and automobiles.
Directions: On US Highway 75 in Hallock.

Walleye Inn Motel
Minnesota Highway 11 W., Baudette, MN 56623
218-634-1550 or 888-634-5944•www.walleyeinn.com

Amenities: High-speed wireless Internet, continental breakfast, non-smoking rooms, suites with Jacuzzi, refrigerators, microwaves, vehicle plug-ins, wheelchair accessible, truck parking, and remote color cable television with free HBO.
Features you'll appreciate: Snowmobile trails nearby and convenient to restaurants.
Directions: On Highway 11 on the western edge of town.

Voyageur Motel
1210 Third Avenue, International Falls, MN 56649
218-283-9424 or 877-283-9424•www.voyageurmotel.net

Amenities: Rooms include wireless Internet, continental breakfast, coffee makers, cable television, and always free coffee.
Features you'll appreciate: Fitness center, library and outdoor plug-ins.

Directions: From the south on US Highway 53, follow Highway 53 N. into International Falls. The motel is on the left, past the Dairy Queen.

Alder Place - The Inn
13 Alder Road, Babbitt, MN 55706
218-827-2220 or 218-827-2113 • www.alderplace.com

Amenities: Ten rooms for one to five people, and common room with fireplace, tables, chairs, piano, and a community kitchen.
Features you'll appreciate: On the edge of the Boundary Waters Canoe Area Wilderness and Superior National Forest, near Birch Lake. Public beach and boat access is a short drive from Alder Place, paved bike and walking trail through pine forest from the edge of town to the beach, snowmobile from the front door to the Stoney Spur Snowmobile trail, and two cross-country ski trails nearby.
Directions: At the edge of Babbitt.

Lakeview Home & Motel
7533 Gold Coast Road, Crane Lake, MN 55725
218-993-2311 or 800-628-4446 • www.lkvmotel.com

Amenities: Private two-bedroom home and three motel rooms. The Lakeview home includes satellite television, full kitchen, full bath, screen porch, and three-season porch, one queen bed, and two double beds — sleeps six; and three guest rooms with one or two bedrooms.
Features you'll appreciate: Boat launch and dock slips with electricity.
Directions: From Orr, head east on County Road 23 (Orr-Buyck Road), which becomes County Road 24. In Buyck, continue heading north on what is now Crane Lake Road. Cross the small bridge in the town of Crane Lake. The home is located one block on the left side of the road and the motel is on the right side.

Royal Shooks Motel

Minnesota highways 1 and 72, Kelliher, MN 56650
218-647-8379 or 888-921-5222•www.paulbunyan.net/users/shookmtl/

Amenities: Guest rooms offer television, courtesy coffee, microwave, refrigerator, shower, and carpeted rooms. Some rooms have kitchenettes, refrigerator, stove, pots, pans, and dishes.
Features you'll appreciate: Handicap accessible, pets are allowed with prior permission, vehicle plug-in available.
Directions: Driving west on Highway 1, continue to the intersection of Highway 1 with Highway 72. Drive north five miles to Kelliher. The motel is in the Waskish area south of Upper Red Lake.

Grand Portage Lodge & Casino

70 Casino Drive, Grand Portage, MN 55605
218-475-2401 or 800-543-1384•www.grandportage.com/rooms.php

Amenities: Double-bedded rooms offer queen-sized beds; single-bedded rooms offer king-sized beds, free high-speed wireless Internet, and access to an indoor heated pool and sauna.
Features you'll appreciate: Suites include parlor room with electric fireplace, whirlpool tub, and wet bar.
Directions: Thirty-five miles north of Grand Marais on Minnesota Highway 61.

Motel Ely — Budget Host

1047 Sheridan Street E., Ely, MN 55731
218-365-3237 or 800-891-0334•www.ely-motels.com

Amenities: Nine guest rooms include wireless high-speed Internet access, continental breakfast, ground-level, at-door parking; cable

television, nonsmoking rooms, free in-room coffee, phones with free local calls, queen-sized beds, and air conditioning.
Features you'll appreciate: Pets allowed and car plug-ins.
Directions: In Ely, hotel is located between S. Tenth Avenue E. and S. Eleventh Avenue E. on Sheridan Street E.

Aspen Lodge
310 E. Minnesota Highway 61, Grand Marais, MN 55604
218-387-2500 or 800-247-6020, ext. 3
www.gmhotel.net/properties.aspenlodge.cfm

Amenities: Swimming pool, whirlpool spa, sauna, and sun deck. Aspen Lodge offers air-conditioned king, king spa, double queen and family suites that include refrigerators, cable television, and free Wi-Fi, free guest laundry and continental breakfast.
Features you'll appreciate: Walk to dining, shops, galleries, and the harbor.
Directions: Heading northeast into Grand Marais on Highway 61, go two blocks past the stoplight. Aspen Lodge is on the Lake Superior side of the highway.

Drake Motel
172 Pine Avenue, Blackduck, MN 56630
218-835-4567 or 888-253-8501 • www.drakemotel.com

Amenities: Thirteen guest rooms, ten of which are standard rooms, two with kitchenettes, and one large unit that can sleep seven, has a full kitchen and can connect with a standard unit for larger parties. Each unit has two double beds, color cable television with HBO, in-room coffee, and air conditioning. Also available: outdoor plug-ins, fish- and game-cleaning room, deep freeze to store fish and game, area to hang deer and bear, gas grill, and picnic area for guests.

Features you'll appreciate: Bait shop, two restaurants, supper club, grocery store, banks, gas stations, movie theater, bowling alley located in a two block radius. Kenneled pets welcomed.
Directions: In Blackduck on US Highway 71. Twenty-four miles north of Bemidji or thirty miles south of Upper Red Lake.

Marjo Motel
710 US Highway 169, Tower, MN 55790
218-753-4851

Amenities: Eight-unit motel in wooded setting with access to Lake Vermilion. Air conditioning and cable television with HBO.
Features you'll appreciate: Nine miles to Fortune Bay Casino, eighteen miles to Giants Ridge, and a quarter-mile to Taconite Trail and walking trails.
Directions: Off Highway 169 at the western entrance to Tower.

Timberwolf Inn
50021 Jack the Horse Road, Marcell, MN 56657
218-832-3990 • www.timberwolfinn.com

Amenities: Twelve rooms with two queen-sized log beds, local television, phone, and a bathtub-shower. Open year round. Snowmobile access to trails.
Features you'll appreciate: Restaurant and lounge.
Directions: Thirty miles north of Grand Rapids on Minnesota Highway 38, also known as Edge of the Wilderness National Scenic Byway.

Chateau Motel
1203 Minnesota Highway 32 N., Red Lake Falls, MN 56750
218-253-4144•www.chateaurlf.com

Amenities: Free high-speed Internet. On-site off-sale liquor store. Most rooms have refrigerator and microwave. Smoking rooms available. Free coffee.

Features you'll appreciate: Truck and large vehicle parking, cold weather hook-ups, pets allowed, copy and fax service, and restaurants nearby.

Directions: Located on the north edge of Red Lake Falls on Highway 32 that runs through town.

Chisholm Inn & Suites
501 Iron Drive, Chisholm, MN 55719
218-254-2000 or 877-255-3156•www.chisholminn.com/p2

Amenities: Guest rooms and suites include access to unlimited wireless access, free breakfast, full-size indoor pool and sauna, small microwave and refrigerators, easy access to trails and wilderness, lobby with fireplace, television and sofas, newspapers, and snacks.

Features you'll appreciate: Borders on the Mesabi Trail containing many miles of continuing trails perfect for snowmobiles, hiking, and biking.

Directions: Right off US Highway 169 on Iron Drive in Chisholm.

Koke's Motel
714 Fayal Road, Eveleth, MN 55734
218-744-4500 or 800-892-5107•http://kokesmotel.com

Amenities: Fourteen air-conditioned rooms, cable television, complimentary coffee and cookies, microwaves, refrigerators, free wireless Internet.

Features you'll appreciate: Parking for buses, trucks, and boat trailers, winter plug-ins, and pets welcome with approval. Two blocks from business district and near the US Hockey Hall of Fame.

Directions: Going north on US Highway 53, take the first exit for Eveleth, take a left and go six blocks. Motel is on the left.

Hibbing Park Hotel & Suites
1402 E. Howard Street, Hibbing, MN 55746
218-262-3481 or 800-262-3481 • www.hibbingparkhotel.com/lodging/

Amenities: 120 guest rooms. Electronic key-card door locks, cable television with Showtime, wireless or wired Internet.
Features you'll appreciate: Indoor pool, sauna, hot tub, and exercise room. Special rates for tour groups. On-site restaurant.
Directions: Just north of Hibbing Community College. Take US Highway 169 heading northeast, turn right on E. Howard Street.

White Oak Inn & Suites
201 Fourth Avenue NW, Deer River, MN 56636
877-633-5504 or 218-246-9400 • www.whiteoakinnandsuites.com

Amenities: Forty-nine guest rooms. Microwaves, refrigerators, high-speed Internet, cable television, in-room coffee, continental breakfast, and non-smoking or smoking rooms.
Features you'll appreciate: Heated swimming pool, kids-only pool, whirlpool, exercise room, tanning room, video game room, laundry facilities, and lobby with fireplace. Dining nearby.
Directions: Off US Highway 2 on Fourth Avenue NW in Deer River. Two blocks west of the intersection of Highway 2 and Minnesota Highway 6.

Whispering Pines Motel
5763 Minnesota Highway 61, Silver Bay, MN 55614
218-226-4712 or 800-332-0531

Amenities: Seven guest units, satellite television, phones, bathtubs or showers, microwaves and refrigerators, in-room coffee. One honeymoon cabin with gas fireplace and three-quarter bath.
Features you'll appreciate: Pets are welcome.
Directions: Five miles northeast of Silver Bay at the junction of Highway 61 and Minnesota Highway 1.

The Northome Motel
12157 County Road 15, Northome, MN 56661
218-897-5216 or 800-263-1770

Amenities: Six guest rooms. Microwaves, refrigerators, televisions, and some rooms with a kitchenette.
Features you'll appreciate: Pets allowed in indoor units. Outdoor plug-ins available. Open fall and winter.
Directions: At the western edge of Northome, at the intersection of Minnesota Highway 46 and US Highway 71 (which runs parallel to Minnesota Highway 1).

Itascan Motel
610 Pokegama Avenue S., Grand Rapids, MN 55744
218-326-3489 or 218-326-8114 or 800-842-7733 • http://itascan.com/

Amenities: Guest rooms offer kitchenettes, air conditioning, cribs, free HBO, fax available, pets welcome, free coffee, and guest laundry.
Features you'll appreciate: Winter plug-ins, and smoking and non-smoking rooms.

Directions: In Grand Rapids on US Highway 169 (Pokegama Avenue S.), between SE Sixth Street and SE Seventh Street.

Lake George Pines Motel
37197 US Highway 71, Lake George, MN 56458
218-266-3914

Amenities: Guest rooms sleep one to six people. All rooms have refrigerators, microwaves, and in-room coffee. Fully equipped kitchens are available.

Features you'll appreciate: Seven miles from Itasca State Park.

Directions: On Highway 71, twenty-nine miles north of Park Rapids and twenty-four miles south of Bemidji.

Flood Bay Motel
1511 Minnesota Highway 61, Two Harbors, MN 55616
218-834-4076

Amenities: Ten guest rooms with lake or woodland view, some with queen beds, air conditioned, all rooms non-smoking.

Features you'll appreciate: Pets not allowed on premises.

Directions: In Two Harbors on Highway 61.

Chase on the Lake
502 Cleveland Boulevard, Walker, MN 56484
888-242-7306 or 218-547-7777 • www.chaseonthelake.com

Amenities: Seventy hotel rooms, ten two- and three-bedroom "condo-tels," indoor pool, sports bar, The 502 Restaurant, Java Loon coffee shop and gelato bar.

Features you'll appreciate: Spa, marina, convention center, bowling alley, and many rentals including boats, bikes, and Sea-Doo personal watercraft.

Directions: Located on the shores of Walker Bay on Leech Lake in downtown Walker.

Grand Inn Moorhead
810 Belsly Boulevard, Moorhead, MN 56560
218-233-7501 • www.grandinnmotels.com

Amenities: Single- and queen-bed rooms, double and single rooms, free breakfast, free wireless high-speed Internet, coffee in lobby, cable television with HBO, and free local phone calls.

Features you'll appreciate: RV and truck parking, parking plug-ins, and pets allowed in smoking rooms.

Directions: From Interstate 94, take Exit 1A and go south two blocks on US Highway 75.

Allyndale Motel
510 N. Sixty-Sixth Avenue W., Duluth, MN 55807
218-628-1061

Amenities: Guest rooms offer kitchenettes with refrigerators, microwaves, free wireless Internet, cable television, and air conditioning. Family and extended-stay suites available.

Features you'll appreciate: Complimentary breakfast on weekends in summer months. Located on five-acre nature setting.

Directions: If heading north on Interstate 35, take Exit 251-A (Cody Street). Turn left at N. Sixty-Sixth Avenue W.; hotel is near the end of the street. If heading south on Interstate 35, take Exit 252 to N. Central Avenue and proceed to Cody Street. Turn right at N. Sixty-Sixth Avenue W. to the motel.

The Inn on Lake Superior
350 Canal Park Drive, Duluth, MN 55802
218-726-1111 or 888-668-4352 • www.theinnonlakesuperior.com

Amenities: 175 rooms. Refrigerators, microwaves, coffeemakers, hair dryers, flat-screen televisions, high-speed wireless Internet access, full-size ironing board and iron, clock radio with MP3 hook-up, breakfast, private balcony or patio overlooking Lake Superior. Pets accepted in designated pet rooms.

Features you'll appreciate: Indoor and outdoor heated pools, complimentary bed and breakfast bar, and nightly outdoor campfires along Lake Superior.

Directions: If heading south on Interstate 35, take Exit 256B, follow Lake Avenue, turn left onto Lake Avenue (Canal Park Drive) and proceed to The Inn on Lake Superior, which will be on your left. **If heading north on** Interstate 35, take Exit 256B, turn right on Canal Park Drive and proceed to The Inn on Lake Superior, on your left.

Moose Lake Motel
125 S. Arrowhead Lane, Moose Lake, MN 55767
218-485-8003 or 888-299-8411 • www.mooselakemotel.com

Amenities: Twelve guest rooms. Air conditioning, direct-dial phones, cable television, refrigerators, microwaves, smoking and non-smoking rooms.

Features you'll appreciate: Internet access and pets are allowed.

Directions: In downtown Moose Lake on S. Arrowhead Lane.

America's Best Value Inn
60671 Minnesota Highway 23, Finlayson, MN 55735
320-245-5284 • www.americasbestvalueinn.com/bestv.cfm?idp=1314

Amenities: Thirty guest rooms, family and Jacuzzi suites, and ADA compliant guest rooms. High-speed wireless Internet, microwaves, mini-refrigerators, hairdryers, iron, ironing board, and wake-up service.
Features you'll appreciate: Guest laundry facility, handicap accessible, limited pets allowed, and truck and bus parking.
Directions: Located east of Interstate 35 at Exit 195 on Highway 23. One-and-a-half hours north of the Twin Cities, and one hour south of Duluth.

Select Inn
821 US Highway 75 N., Breckenridge, MN 56520
218-643-9201 or 800-641-1000

Amenities: Twenty-seven guest rooms, king- or queen-sized beds, indoor pool, whirlpool, video games, vending machines, continental breakfast, and free high-speed Internet.
Features you'll appreciate: Whirlpool (centrally located), laundry facilities, accessible to disabled, pets allowed.
Directions: From Fergus Falls go west twenty-three miles on Minnesota Highway 210 to Breckenridge.

Old Oak Inn
920 Main Street S., Pine City, MN 55063
800-524-2512 or 320-629-2511 • www.oldoakinn.net

Amenities: Eleven motel rooms with one queen bed or two double beds, four suites with kitchenettes, four hostel rooms, cable television, microwaves, and refrigerators in all rooms, complimentary coffee, and coffee and rolls on weekends.

Features you'll appreciate: Disabled accessible rooms, non-smoking and smoking rooms, pets allowed, laundry facilities, wireless high-speed Internet access from lobby, gas barbeque grill, patio, decks, and picnic tables for guest use.

Directions: From Interstate 35, take Exit 169 and go east on Minnesota Highway 324. The Inn is on Main Street S. between Hillside Avenue SW and Johnson Avenue SW.

Resorts

Warroad Estates Marina
156 Lakeview Drive, Warroad, MN 56763
218-386-2200•www.warroadestatesmarina.com

Amenities: Cabins have electric floor heat, dishwasher, disposal, air conditioning, and patio grill. Each cabin sleeps six; rollaway beds are available.

Features you'll appreciate: Eighteen-hole golf course and 500 miles of groomed snowmobile trails nearby, on Lake of the Woods, Westgate Marina, and 7 Clans Warroad Casino.

Directions: One mile north of Warroad on Minnesota Highway 313.

Adrian's Resort
3362 Red Oak Road NW, Baudette, MN 56623
218-634-1985•http://adriansresort.net

Amenities: Housekeeping cabins are furnished with linens, towels, and dishes; ice fish house sleepers, grocery, bait, tackle, and on- and off-sale liquor, licenses, and fish cleaning also available.

Features you'll appreciate: Golf, driving range, and casino nearby. Snowmobiles are welcome.

Directions: From Baudette, twelve miles northwest on Minnesota Highway 172.

Bayview Lodge
1609 Twenty-Sixth Avenue NW, Baudette, MN 56623
218-634-2194•www.bayviewlakeofthewoods.com

Amenities: Waterfront cabins include beds, furniture, fully equipped kitchens, linens, and towels, electric heat, and cable TV.

Features you'll appreciate: Boat landing, docking facilities, rental boats, bait, tackle, fishing and hunting licenses, groceries, pop, and snacks.

Directions: Six-and-a-half miles northwest of Baudette on Minnesota Highway 172.

Camp Idlewood

3033 County Road 20, International Falls, MN 56649
218-286-5551 or 888-741-1228 • www.campidlewood.com

Amenities: One- to three-bedroom cabins with vaulted ceilings and knotty pine interiors, boat and canoe rentals, sauna, playground, and sand beach.

Features you'll appreciate: Surrounded by Voyageurs National Park, dock spaces available, and snowmobile and bike trails. Pets welcome.

Directions: Six miles east of International Falls.

Island View Lodge

1817 Minnesota Highway 11 E., International Falls, MN 56649
218-286-3511 or 800-777-7856 • www.gotorainylake.com

Amenities: One- to six-bedroom cabins, lodge rooms, satellite TV in all lodge rooms, restaurant, lounge, sauna, marina and docks with electrical service, playground, beach, and guide services.

Features you'll appreciate: Wireless Internet, pontoon, fishing boat, motor rentals, live bait, ice; fish cleaned, wrapped and frozen; oil, gasoline, fishing maps, and tackle. Pets welcome.

Directions: Twelve miles east of International Falls at the entrance to Voyageurs National Park.

Carlson's Harmony Beach Resort

10002 Gappa Road, Kabetogama, MN 56669
218-875-2811 • www.harmonybeachresort.com

Amenities: Twelve lake-view or lake-access cabins with shower, linens, fully equipped kitchen, deck with furniture, picnic table, and grill.

Features you'll appreciate: On Lake Kabetogama. Beach, dock, boat, paddle boat, funyak, playground, basketball, volleyball, bait, tackle, ice, gas, fish cleaning and fish packaging. Hiking, snowmobiling, and cross-country skiing nearby.

Directions: On the edge of Voyageurs National Park and the south shore of Lake Kabetogama.

October Ridge Resort
66211 County Road 31, Northome, MN 56661
218-897-5957 or 888-654-2541 • www.octoberridgeresort.com

Amenities: Five cabins and one mobile home. All units have fully equipped kitchens with appliances, tubs, and showers.

Features you'll appreciate: On Island Lake. Playground, volleyball, sandy beach, croquet, basketball, horseshoes, paddle boats, fire pit, pontoon, firewood, bait, fish-cleaning house, gas, ice fishing, and snowmobile trails. Golf, casino, and downhill skiing nearby.

Directions: Thirty miles from Big Winnie and Upper Red Lake.

Whispering Winds
9084 Little Sweden Road, Cook, MN 55723
218-666-5699 or 800-964-6306 • www.whisperingwindsresort.com

Amenities: Seven cabins each with sundeck, deck furniture, electricity, heat, showers, equipped kitchen, and linens.

Features you'll appreciate: Sandy beach, hiking, horseshoes, bait, tackle, gas, oil, fish cleaning, fish freezing, grills, water skiing, canoe, and paddle boat. Golf, tennis, movie theater, laundry, and fine dining nearby.

Directions: On the western end of Lake Vermilion, take County Highway 24 (Vermilion Drive) to Little Swapper Road to Little Sweden Road.

Daisy Bay Resort
4070 County Road 77, Tower, MN 55790
218-753-4958 or 800-449-8306 • www.daisybay.com

Amenities: Ten cabins, each with microwaves, coffee makers, TVs, VCR, DVD player, lawn furniture, and grill. All cabins furnished for light housekeeping.

Features you'll appreciate: On Lake Vermilion. Dorothy Molter Museum, International Wolf Center, Minnesota Discovery Center, mailboat excursions, Mineview in the Sky, Soudan Underground Mine State Park, Orr Bogwalk, Tower Train Museum, Vince Shute Wildlife Sanctuary and The Wilderness at Fortune Bay golf course nearby.

Directions: From Interstate 35 take Exit 235 to Cloquet by way of Minnesota Highway 33, then take US Highway 53 to US Highway 169, and go east eighteen miles to County Road 77, which curves around Daisy Bay in Lake Vermilion. Go seven miles and make a right just after Clover Point Road and go two miles to the resort.

Timertown Resort
25601 Timertown Drive NW, Shevlin, MN 56676
218-243-2713 • www.timertownresort.com

Amenities: Five efficiency apartments, each with full kitchen, refrigerator, private bath, shower, and open living-dining area.

Features you'll appreciate: Screened fish-cleaning house with running water and double sink, in the woods.

Directions: Timertown Resort is west of Debs, thirty miles northwest of Bemidji, in northwestern Minnesota.

Eagle Ridge Resort
Stallion Court NE, Tenstrike, MN 56683
218-586-2700 or 800-279-5177 • http://eagleridgeresort.net

Amenities: Seven cabins with showers, linens, fully equipped kitchens, fire rings, grills, and picnic tables.
Features you'll appreciate: On Gull Lake. Private beach, game room, bait, tackle, gas, firewood, boat, paddle boat, canoe, and pontoon. Hiking, shopping, and golf nearby. Pets welcome.
Directions: From Bemidji, follow US Highway 71 north to Turtle River. Turn left onto Minnesota Highway 23. Go five-and-a-half miles and turn right at the Eagle Ridge Resort sign.

White Birch Resort
Blackduck, MN 56630
218-835-4552 or 877-835-4552 • www.whitebirchresort.net

Amenities: Nine lodging units, including two 3,000-square-foot reunion homes that sleep up to twenty-two people. All cabins have lake views, equipped kitchens, cable TV, grills, and fire pits.
Features you'll appreciate: Heated pool, volleyball set, swimming beach, playground, basketball court, horseshoes, arcade, fitness equipment, boat and pontoon rentals, Internet, ATV trails nearby, and ice house rentals.
Directions: Three miles west of Blackduck and twenty-seven miles northeast of Bemidji on the north shore of Blackduck Lake.

Arcadia Lodge
52001 County Road 284, Bigfork, MN 56628
218-832-3852 or 888-832-3852 • www.arcadialodge.com

Amenities: Twenty-one cabins and three motel-style lodge units. All cabins have air conditioning, satellite TV, equipped kitchens, shower and tub. Some units have gas fireplaces, and each cabin has its own deck or screen porch.

Features you'll appreciate: On Big Turtle Lake. Each unit has patio tables and chairs or a picnic table, and charcoal grill. Other features: wireless Internet, sandy beach, basketball, horseshoes, game room, kayaks, canoes, paddle boats, pontoon, tubing, waterskiing, and gift shop.

Directions: From Grand Rapids, take Minnesota Highway 38 north twenty-eight miles to Marcell. Take County Road 286 for three miles to W. Turtle Lake Road. Turn right and continue three miles.

Kokomo Resort

48301 Minnesota Highway 38, Marcell, MN 56657

218-832-3774 or 888-848-7407 • www.kokomoresort.com

Amenities: Seven lakeside cabins. All cabins have satellite TV, linens, and fully equipped kitchens.

Features you'll appreciate: On North Star Lake. Grill, outdoor furniture, and fire pit at each cabin. Wireless Internet, sandy beach, playground, paddleboat, canoe, basketball, horseshoes, volleyball, hiking trails, trampoline, swim raft, game room, and gift shop.

Directions: Twenty-six miles north of Grand Rapids and two miles from Marcell.

The Lodge at Giants Ridge

6373 Wynne Creek Drive, County Road 138, Biwabik, MN 55708

218-865-7170 or 877-442-6877

www.lodgeatgiantsridge.com

Amenities: Sixty-seven suites, many of which include fireplaces and double whirlpool spas. All suites have bath separate from private sleeping room and kitchenette.

Features you'll appreciate: Wireless Internet, fine dining, heated indoor pool, hot tub, outdoor pool, members-only beach, fitness center, tennis and volleyball courts, ski-in and -out access, game room, and laundry.

Directions: Take US Highway 169 west to Tower. Turn left on Minnesota Highway 135 to Aurora. Turn right, continuing on Highway 135 for two miles. Turn right onto County Road 138 for three miles. The Lodge at Giants Ridge will be on your left.

Fenstad's Resort

6572 Minnesota Highway 61, Little Marais, MN 55614

218-226-4724 • http://fenstadsresort.com

Amenities: Sixteen lakeshore cabins with fully equipped kitchens, shower, and linens. Nine have fireplaces.

Features you'll appreciate: On Lake Superior's North Shore. Gravel beach, boat harbor, docks, kayak, and hiking trails.

Directions: On the lake side of Highway 61 a few miles northeast of Little Marais.

Dreamers Resort

16585 Wilkey Loop Road NE, Bemidji, MN 56601

218-751-1020 or 866-223-7326 • http://dreamersresort.com

Amenities: Eight cabins with refrigerators, microwaves, toasters, coffee pots, pans, silverware, dishes, cups, and glasses. One cabin has a fenced, private yard for pets.

Features you'll appreciate: On Big Lake with fishing guide service. Boats, gas, bait, ice, candy, pop, and ice cream.

Directions: From Bemidji, take County Road 12 (Piwer Dam Road NE) about ten miles east of Bemidji. Take Forest Route Road until it turns into Wilkey Route Road NE.

Sah-Kah-Tay Beach Resort
16348 Sixtieth Avenue NW, Cass Lake, MN 56633
218-335-2424 or 800-232-3224 • www.sahkahtay.com

Amenities: Twelve cabins with kitchen appliances, satellite TV, picnic table, charcoal grills, and one dock space.

Features you'll appreciate: On Cass Lake, guide service, fish cleaning, ice fishing, snowmobiling, free boat launching and use of paddle boats, gas, oil, life jackets, and freezer space. Pets welcome.

Directions: Three-fourths of a mile north of the town of Cass Lake on Sixtieth Aveue.

Ball Club Lake Lodge
34858 County Road 39, Deer River, MN 56636
218-246-8908 or 218-360-0496
www.ballclublakelodge.com

Amenities: Five cabins each with lake views, utensils, coffee makers, bedding, picnic table, microwave oven, and gas grill.

Features you'll appreciate: On Ball Club Lake. Beach, play equipment, boat, and fishing. Children's Discovery Museum, Forest History Center, Judy Garland Museum, casino, golf, trail rides, and Grand Rapids Speedway nearby.

Directions: From Deer River, go west on US Highway 2 for about eight miles. Turn right onto County Road 39 and go about two and one-half miles north.

Vallhalla Resort
24218 E. Island Lake Road, Detroit Lakes, MN 56501
218-847-8753 • http://detroitlakes.com/valhalla

Amenities: Eight cabins each with screen porch and private dock. Choice of completely modern or semi-modern log cabins. All cabins furnished for light housekeeping.

Features you'll appreciate: On Island Lake. Tackle, bait, boats, fish-cleaning house, fish freezing, gas, oil, and laundry. Beach with diving raft, canoes, kayaks, playground, and horseshoe pit. Hiking trails, Itasca State Park, restaurants, golf courses, and amusement parks nearby.

Directions: Twenty miles northeast of Detroit Lakes, twenty-seven miles west of Park Rapids.

The Hideaway Resort

25574 E. Island Lake Road, Detroit Lakes, MN 56501

218-847-6886 or 800-363-7122•http://detroitlakes.com/hideaway/

Amenities: Seven lakeside cabins with a sandy beach; one, two, and three bedrooms; full cooking capability: utensils, dishes, pots and pans, microwave, coffee pot, toaster; color televisions, and bed linens are provided; thermostatically controlled heat; showers; baby cribs, rollaways, and highchairs upon request.

Features you'll appreciate: The Tamarac National Wildlife Refuge is located a few miles away, offering trails for hiking and birdwatching. Golf courses within thirty miles, supper clubs, craft and antique shops close by, and casino and nightclub forty-five miles away.

Directions: Midway between Park Rapids and Detroit Lakes, five miles off the intersection of Minnesota Highway 34 and County Road 37.

Little Norway Resort

32016 Little Mantrap Drive, Park Rapids, MN 56470

218-732-5480•www.littlenorwayresort.com

Amenities: Two types of cottages: wood frame with cathedral ceilings and two baths, or modified A-frame. All cabins are paneled in pine, have lake views and are only a few feet from the shore. Each cabin has a fully equipped kitchen with appliances, shower, cable TV, linens, deck with chairs, charcoal grill, and campfire ring.

Features you'll appreciate: On Little Mantrap Lake. Lodge has wireless Internet, preschool play room, family area with books, board games, movies, game room with pool table, ping pong, and video games. Pontoon and boat rental available. Free canoe, paddle boat, and kayaks. Beach with gazebo and anchored swim raft.

Directions: One mile south of Itasca State Park and sixteen miles north of Park Rapids on US Highway 71. From Highway 71, take Little Mantrap Drive; the resort is at the end of the road.

Adventure North Resort
4444 Point Landing Drive NW, Walker, MN 56484
218-547-1532 or 800-294-1532•www.adventurenorthresort.com

Amenities: One-, two-, and three-bedroom cabins, rentals, swimming pool, and sandy beach.

Features you'll appreciate: Wireless Internet, horseback riding, ATV rentals, hiking and biking, playground with merry-go-round, shuffle board, volleyball, horseshoe pit, eagle viewing, and jet skiing. Shopping nearby.

Directions: From Walker, take Minnesota Highway 200 about six miles east to Minnesota Highway 13 (Onigum Road NW) for about six and one-half miles, following the curve around the lake then going north on Pine Point Road NW for about two miles.

Acorn Hill Family Resort and Fishing Lodge
4691 Acorn Hill Lane NW, Walker, MN 56484
218-547-1015 or 800-237-1015•www.acornhill.com

Amenities: Lodge, game room, pavilion, lunch counter, tackle, gas and bait. Protected harbor with boat, motor, and pontoon rentals. One-, two-, and three-bedroom cabins with knotty pine interiors, carpeting, and hardwood floors, RV sites and hookups. Pets welcome.

Features you'll appreciate: Wireless Internet, swimming pool, Jacuzzi, beach, water slide and trampoline, kayaks, fishing and hunting guides, and pro-fishing seminars.

Directions: From Walker, take Minnesota Highway 200 about six miles east to Minnesota Highway 13 (Onigum Road NW) for about six and one-half miles, following the curve around the lake then going north on Pine Point Road NW for about two miles. Turn right on Pinepoint Lane and right again on Acorn Hill Lane NW.

Sievers Resort
Hackensack, MN 56452
218-675-6665•http://sieversresort.com/

Amenities: All seven cabins are paneled, insulated, carpeted, and furnished. Each has TV, a DVD player, electric heat, hot water, fully equipped kitchen, appliances, bed linens, ceiling fans, microwave ovens, and a private dock.

Features you'll appreciate: On private Poquet Lake. Hiking trails, paved roads for biking and rollerblading, Frisbee golf course, golf chipping course, basketball and tennis court, canoe, paddleboat, swim raft, pontoon and motor rental, and boat launching. Each unit comes with a fourteen-foot Lund boat.

Directions: One-fourth mile south of Hackensack on Minnesota Highway 371.

Little Ponderosa Resort
2916 Diamond Crest Road NE, Longville, MN 56655
218-363-2600 or 888-657-0151•www.littleponderosaresort.com

Amenities: Nine cabins with microwaves, coffee makers, showers, and linens.

Features you'll appreciate: On Lake Wabedo. Horseshoes, beach, and playground. Fishing boat, kayak, paddle boat, and pontoon rental available. Golf, turtle races, mini golf, tennis, volleyball, shopping, antiques, souvenirs, bait shops, grocery, and churches nearby.
Directions: From Longville, take Minnesota Highway 84 to County Road 7 then on to County Road 54 NE for about four miles. Then take Wabedo Road for nearly a mile; the road goes by several names as it wraps around the lake: Stoney Creek Road NE, Postal Bay Road, Township Road C. Turn right at County Road C (Diamond Crest Road NE) and go about a mile.

Inn on Gitchegumee
8517 Congdon Boulevard, North Shore Scenic Drive, Duluth, MN 55804
218-525-4979 or 800-317-4979•www.innongitchegumee.com

Amenities: Ten cabins, each with TV, DVD, charcoal grill, microwave, refrigerator, phone, wireless Internet, air conditioning, tub, shower, linens, deck or balcony, playground, and bonfire pit.
Features you'll appreciate: Views of Lake Superior. Themed suites with handmade quilts. Parks, golf, hiking, tennis courts, public gardens, beach nearby, snowmobile and cross-country skiing tails.
Directions: Nine miles from downtown Duluth and eighteen miles from Two Harbors on the North Shore Scenic Drive (Old Highway 61).

Park Lake Resort
2243 County Road 7, Mahtowa, MN 55707
218-389-6935 or 800-315-6935•www.parklakeresort.com

Amenities: Four furnished cabins; two are seasonal. Year-round cabins are lakeside with wraparound decks and gas fireplaces. TV, shower, tub, and equipped kitchen.

Features you'll appreciate: On Park Lake. Bar and restaurant on site. Fishing and snowmobiling. Casino nearby.
Directions: Thirty miles south of Duluth or forty-five miles north of Hinckley on County Road 7.

Sand Lake Resort
94154 County Highway 61, Sturgeon Lake, MN 55783
218-485-8164 or 877-314-9252 • www.sandlakeresort.com

Amenities: Eight cabins with LCD TV, DVD, shower, linens, and fully equipped kitchen.
Features you'll appreciate: On Sand Lake. Wireless Internet, boat, pontoon, paddle boat, canoeing, biking, hiking, game room, and fire pit. Golf and casinos nearby.
Directions: Located on County Highway 61, just south of W. County Line Road, between Moose Lake and Sturgeon Lake.

Waldheim Resort
9096 Waldheim Drive, Finlayson, MN 55735
320-233-7405 or 888-925-3434 • www.waldheimresort.com

Amenities: Five cabins, each with shower, tub, linens, and fully equipped kitchen.
Features you'll appreciate: On Big Pine Lake. Movie rental, bait, gas, and gift shop. Cinnamon rolls and newspaper delivered on Sunday mornings. Biking, canoeing, kayaking, horseback riding, hiking, laundry, kennel, groceries, museums, casinos, and bowling nearby. Pet friendly in three cabins.
Directions: One hour south of Duluth or one-and-a-half hours north of the Twin Cities in Pine County. From Finlayson, take County Road 18 west to Sprandel Road and turn at Waldheim Lane.

Spritual and
Educational
Retreats

WindCradle Retreat
2909 E. Minnesota Highway 61, Grand Marais, MN 55604
218-387-1536 or 866-586-2224•www.windcradle.org

What you'll find: Created in 2008, WindCradle provides a setting for soul, mind, and body restoration. Amenities include a guest house, an on-site outdoor sauna, and a labyrinth. Also available: spiritual direction, massages, a small prayer chapel with lake view, connecting trails from WindCradle to the Superior Hiking Trail, beach combing, hiking, reflecting, and gathering spaces with stunning Lake Superior views. You can sign up for an upcoming retreat, or contact WindCradle to design a retreat for your own group.
Directions: Eight miles northeast of Grand Marais on Highway 61.

Sisters of Saint Benedict Mount Saint Benedict Monastery
620 Summit Avenue, Crookston MN 56716
218-281-3441•www.msb.net

What you'll find: The Mount Saint Benedict Center provides a space for individual retreats for prayer, spiritual growth, personal journaling, or spiritual guidance, as well as a place for groups to reflect on scripture or ministry. Workshops also are available. Overnight accommodations are available for up to seventy-nine people, and dining options are available for groups of up to 200. Walking paths, a nature trail, and gardens also offer a chance to slip away and enjoy solitude.
Directions: From US Highway 2 in downtown Crookston, go east on E. Fifth Street and continue on Riverside Street to Summit Avenue.

Pathways

502 Beltrami Avenue NW, No. 3, Bemidji, MN 56619
218-751-4208 • www.pathwaysbiblecamps.com

What you'll find: Pathways, a Bible camp corporation of the Evangelical Lutheran Church in America, offers programs and retreats year-round for individuals, families, and youth. Family resort weekends, mother-daughter and women of faith scrapbooking weekends, and an annual memorial golf scramble are among faith-building opportunities. Pathways has three locations in northern Minnesota: Baudette, Menahga, and Cass Lake.

Directions: Contact the camp for directions, depending on which camp is chosen.

Turning Point Retreat Center

725 SW Fourth Avenue, Grand Rapids, MN 55744 (mailing address)
9191 Hakola Road, Hibbing, MN 55746 (physical address)
218-326-1939 • www.turningpointretreat.net

What you'll find: Looking for a place in northern Minnesota for a family reunion? A spiritual retreat? Or a women's scrapbooking weekend? Turning Point Retreat Center offers Christian hospitality on 160 acres and a four-season lodge for people of all faiths. A quiet lake and three miles of hiking trails are among the natural highlights. Turning Point is open year-round.

Directions: Take Minnesota Highway 73 south of Hibbing to County Road 184/Floodwood River Road and turn right; turn right again on Hakola Road/Township Road 5183.

Smokey Hills Wilderness Retreat
53014 Minnesota Highway 34, Osage, MN 56570
320-761-4863 • www.smokeyhills.com

What you'll find: You'll find it easy to stay busy at Smokey Hills Wilderness Retreat near Park Rapids. Whether it's a church spiritual retreat, a family reunion, a weekend of fishing and ATV-riding, or crafting and scrapbooking, Smokey Hills can meet your needs. A conference center is available and is equipped with a sound booth, screen, and projection; catering facilities and restaurant; and private and group lodging .

Directions: Along Highway 34 twenty-five miles east of Detroit Lakes or nine miles west of Park Rapids.

McCabe Renewal Center
2125 Abbotsford Avenue, Duluth, MN 55803
218-724-5266
www.duluthbenedictines.org/ministries/mccabe-renewal-center/

What you'll find: The gracious beauty of a Georgian-style mansion built in 1914 is part of what makes the McCabe Renewal Center special. Operating as a retreat since 1977, it is run by the Benedictine sisters. The former home of a Duluth grain merchant offers space for spiritual and personal growth, for personal or group retreats, workshops, or other gatherings. Members of all faith groups and traditions are welcome, and all workshops and retreats have a suggested donation for costs incurred. Some overnight accommodations are available.

Directons: From downtown Duluth, take Interstate 35 to London Road and go slight left at S. Twenty-Sixth Avenue E.; turn right at E. Fourth Street, take the first left onto Wallace Avenue, turn left at E. Arrowhead Road, take the third right onto Columbus Avenue, take the second left onto W. Lewis St., and then the first right onto Abbotsford.

One Heartland Center
26001 Heinz Road, Willow River, MN 55795
888-545-6658 • http://oneheartlandcenter.com

What you'll find: Serenity and tranquility in the northern woods— that's what One Heartland Center (formerly Camp Heartland) will provide you. The center offers overnight accommodations for groups of up to 150 and for day retreat groups of several hundred. Since 1993, Camp Heartland has helped improve the lives of children, young people, and their families who are affected by HIV/AIDS and other significant life challenges. Rental of One Heartland Center helps fund summer camping programs and year-round support of children and families facing life with HIV/AIDS, transitional housing, foster care, and other isolating circumstances.

Directions: Take Interstate 35 to Exit 205 for Willow River/Bruno, turn left at County Road 43 and left again at County Highway 61. Take the second right onto Long Lake Road, right on Heinz Road and right again on Margolis Trail.

Country Garden Retreat
121 Lady Luck Drive, Hinckley, MN 55037
320-384-6052 • http://countrygardenretreat.com

What you'll find: Country Garden Retreat is spacious and sunny, located right next to Hinckley's Grand National Golf Course and down the road from St. Croix State Park. It's ideal for groups of scrapbookers, quilters, or other crafters, as well as for business meetings or church retreats—anyone who wants a comfortable meeting space in a homey atmosphere. Specialized crafting tools (Circuit personal cutting machines, Sizzix die cutters, Rowenta Steam generator iron), high-speed Internet, satellite television, and dry-erase boards are available for the many different groups that visit.

The facility also includes a large studio with tables and chairs for crafts, meetings, and breakout sessions, as well as a spacious kitchen and accommodations for overnight guests.

Directions: From Interstate 35, take Exit 183 and go east on Minnesota Highway 48 (Fire Monument Road), then right on Lady Luck Drive.

Index

278